DISCOVERING THE BEST VERSION OF YOU

THE PATH TO THE BEST YOU

PAM KURT

ALONG WITH 15 OTHER INSPIRING WOMEN AUTHORS

Table of Contents

INTRODUCTION

This book has come about through *Best Version of You*.

It's the company that I started during COVID to empower women. The mission of Best Version of You is to empower, educate, and support women to encourage the mindset and growth to be the best version of themselves, taking everyone to the next level and feeling complete and at peace. It's about collaboration, not competition. This is done through coaching, seminars, programs, trainings, literature, and example.

Best Version of You (BVU) is currently offering: Coaching, affiliate coaching, speaking, training, community support, events, memberships, authorships, merchandise, and community

Signature Coaching Program:

Dream.
Believe.
Achieve.
DBA: YOU!

This program is in three parts. First, to Dream limitless; Second, Believe and develop the mindset, faith, and tools to get you where you want to be; and Third, to Achieve and maintain through self care and tools. If you Dream, Believe, and Achieve, you will be "DBA" as the authentic YOU!

This book is an example of our core values and mission at Best Version of You. A group of women come together to empower women and take them to the next level, and as such this book is a collaboration among a group of women to share their own stories and struggles.

A PATH TO THE BEST YOU

Did you know we are only born with two fears? Just two—the fear of falling, and the fear of loud noises.

Every single other fear, including the unknown, is learned.

Choosing to become the best version of yourself means confronting learned fears. Learned behaviors. Coping mechanisms. Defensive tactics. Communication patterns.

The list goes on.

It's not for the faint of heart.

And that's why you're here—because you're *not* faint of heart. Because you have the courage to find out what could be beyond this next mountain, or hill, or curve in the river.

Becoming the best version of yourself demands authenticity. It demands humility. It demands patience and grace. You became who you are because of the choices you made, with the information you had at that specific moment in time. One of the most important boundaries you must draw for yourself is not judging your past self for information you didn't have at the time when you made a pivotal choice.

You weren't stupid—you were inexperienced.

You weren't a sucker—you were naïve.

You weren't a bad leader—you lacked the wisdom that came from experience.

However you would fill in that blank for yourself, it's important to think back to your past self and thank her. Thank her for doing the best she could with what she had. Thank her for protecting you so you could get to this point in time. Thank her for working so hard for you—her future. Tell her it's okay to be afraid of making the wrong call again—because you will. Every mistake is an opportunity to learn how to do it better, so you can become the best version of you.

In these pages, it is my deepest hope you will find stories of encouragement, of hope, of laughter, and of motivation for those moments when you do want to give up. When you do want to curl back under the blankets because you just can't do it another day. Because all of us have been there.

Becoming your best self, my friend, is a profound act of courage, because you're not just facing down being afraid of the dark or loud sounds. You're facing down every fear you've picked up along the way. You're an amazing, beautiful, conquering warrior.

Fight on, friend. Fight on.

Coach Pamela

This book is dedicated to my son, Joshua Villalta,
for being the reason to never give up.

Pamela Kurt

Best Version of You
Coach

https://www.linkedin.com/in/pamela-kurt-41a26ba/
https://www.facebook.com/pam.kurt
https://www.instagram.com/best_version_you/?hl=en
https://pamkurt.com/
https://bestversionyou.com/

Pamela D. Kurt is an attorney and professional womens' life coach. She received her associate degree, bachelor's degree, Master's in Public Administration and Juris Doctorate in December of 2003. She lives in Ohio with her husband and two black labs. She also enjoys time with her adult son and grandson.

As a professional, Pam has added several additional certifications and advanced training. As an attorney, her area of practice is in family law and juvenile law.

Pam is a very active business owner in her community, and as a result, has held multiple leadership roles, including as a board member and advisor for several nonprofits and agencies. She also recently was named the Leader of the Year for Lake County, 2022.

Through her community involvement and personal passion to empower women, she created a new company: Best Version of You, LLC. This company is to empower and elevate women to their next level and be the best version of themselves. It is about collaboration and not competition. You can reach her at pam@bestversionyou.com or https://pamkurt.com.

EACH CHAPTER HOLDS A GIFT

By Pamela Kurt

"Life is like a book. There are good chapters, and there are bad chapters. But when you get to a bad chapter, you don't stop reading the book! If you do…then you never get to find out what happens next!" – Brian Falkner

As I sit to write this chapter, I am humbled and honored to be part of another anthology that is compiled of so many strong, amazing women. We each have our own struggles, but to be a part of a group of like-minded, strong women is more powerful than one can imagine.

How do you become the best version of yourself? Everyone has their own path and their own story. This is why it's important to share yours. Someone will find inspiration and hope simply because you made it. Sometimes, as we go through life, we think we have no choice, but there is always a choice, and you should be proud to make it!

I always thought that my story would have a happy ending. I felt as if all would be great after the struggle, that you just push through and then, at the end of all of your hard work, there is happiness. Well, life happens. Each life has multiple chapters and stories and as you get older, you realize there is even more to live, more to fight for, and more to appreciate. And you wonder, *How do those chapters all fit together for a happy life?*

I have shared the story of my childhood before. I grew up in a rural community and my father passed away in a car accident when I was eight years old. My mother shortly remarried—they are still married and I got another brother out of the deal, too. But my mother and I didn't get along, so I left the house at 18 years old. College was hard because I didn't have the money to pay for it and didn't know how to get any assistance. So I continued to work to make money for school, and ended up in the Washington, D.C. area for work, which is where I met my ex-husband. There were so many chapters in my young life. I thought when I met my ex-husband that I had found my happy ending.

He was charming, good-looking, and very complimentary. I thought it was great, but when we got married, things changed. He was controlling, and later that turned into abuse. I was divorced and a single mother by 25, still hadn't finished college, and wasn't financially stable. Another chapter of my life, and where is the happy ending? I had so much more to live and learn.

After my divorce, I worked hard to provide for myself and my child and assumed that I would work and that was the end of the story. I would achieve this "best me" and "best life." I also set a timeline for the chapters and stories of my life.

I thought I would be the best me once I reached 18 years old, then again once I got married and had the baby, and again once I got divorced and graduated from college.

I went to college and earned my associate's, bachelor's, master's, and juris doctorate. Looking back, I'm not sure how I did all of that while raising my son, but I made it work.

I thought, *Now I am set, I made it…* but there were years between me graduating, passing the bar, and ultimately opening my own practice, because I didn't believe in myself.

I worked many jobs to make ends meet for most of my life. One of those was working as a substitute teacher. Once I decided to open my open practice, I didn't let go of the side jobs—I had so much doubt. And I said, "God, if this is what I am supposed to do, let me know." I remember this prayer as clear as day.

I was heading to another teaching assignment and knew I had to get back to the law office to do some drafting for a client. But I was afraid to let go and trust God. I was teaching during the day and doing as much legal work as possible at night. And when I came into the office the next day, the phones didn't stop ringing and there was work—plenty of work. So much so that I had to hire interns and paralegals to help me. My practice took off and things started to fall into place. I had to decline teaching assignments because I was already scheduled for court and with clients. I found the answer and followed that calling.

So, another hurdle cleared. Once I open my own practice, I will be the best version of myself. That's it...NOW I made it. But life changes, goals change, and being the best me is an ongoing process.

This January it will be 15 years since I opened my own law practice. Even those 15 years have had many highs and lows. What started as me and a few part-time helpers and interns has grown to over 15 attorneys, four offices, and support staff. I thought if I proved to myself I could do it that would lead to the best me. Ok, now I made it!

Now, life looks different. I got remarried to a college friend, and that was another struggle. He is an alcoholic, and that life is harder than one would ever imagine. So once he gets sober, I can start working on the best me. Well, that didn't work either.

I started looking at the office and my career. I did enjoy helping people, but as lawyers, staff, and clients came and went, I realized that I was giving so much of myself that there was barely anything left for me.

I finally identified my biggest weakness: I would give more than the person receiving; I cared more about their well-being than they did. So, I thought, *What an eye-opener, NOW I can be the best me...*

However, after more prayer and reflection, I realized that every day I need to try to be the best me. Every day presents an opportunity to be the best me. I need to take the time to figure out what that looks like each day.

There are rare, very rare chances that there is that ONE long race, and then you "made it." There are some challenges in life that, once conquered, will make you clearly feel as if you made it. But life needs to be valued and treated as precious as it is. Funny, I thought only old people said things like that...

For me, the BEST VERSION OF MYSELF is a work in progress. As my life and seasons change, as I move on to the next chapter of my life, I can make it through with the help of God, and if I continue to be grateful daily and do his will, I will ALWAYS be the best me and have the best life.

But what makes *you* happy? What makes your heart smile and gives you that warm feeling inside? What are you passionate about? It does change through the years. Sometimes, taking time for self-reflection and looking at the different areas of your life brings some of the answers. Has it changed over the years?

One way to start your own path to being your best self is to answer this magical question: *If money and time were not an object, what would you do?*

As an attorney, I do a lot of family law—divorce, child support and custody, etc. I asked this question of my clients for years. It helps me and the client focus on their wanted outcomes and goals of the case and provides them with some hope for the future. I started using it for myself, too.

And then one day, I asked this *magical question* to a client that was getting her third divorce at 76 years old. Why not? I figured we all need to focus positively on the future.

Her response was that she wanted to be an astronaut. What the hell? I was a little thrown off. Usually when I ask this question, my client has a desire to go back to school or spend more time with her children or advance her current career. I can usually be a good cheerleader for those types of goals, and quickly come up with a timeline and plan to achieve them. But...a 76-year-old who wants to be an astronaut?

This made me stop and slow down. There's always more to what we say we want, right? I asked her why. Why an astronaut? Her response was that she wanted to watch the stars, feel lifeless, and be able to float.

This made my brain take off. I could still help her get to her goals. Long story short, she took an astronomy class, bought a telescope, and her grandson took her to Orlando for a NASA simulation. She met her goal. She wasn't an astronaut, but she was able to achieve the parts that were rewarding to her.

I know we have all heard that it's about the journey. It really is…but we have to start with those goals and THINK BIG!

If money and time were no object, what would you do? What would you wake up and be? Work to try to achieve *those* goals. I bet that on your journey to reach them, you learn more than you would have ever imagined about your own journey and more. Each step of your journey is your own chapter of your own book.

Sometimes, that journey is more valuable than when you finally get to the goal. And sometimes, God is just pointing in that direction to get us on that path and our perceived goal isn't really the goal. God has something even better for us at the end.

So as you start your journey to become your best you, take your time. Do what you want to do and make it count. You deserve to be happy and free. Get that tribe of women to support you on your journey and as you go along, you are becoming the best you!

My wish to you is that every day your journey starts positively and ends positively as you continue each chapter and the steps to becoming your best you.

DREAM. BELIEVE. ACHIEVE.

Love,
Coach Pamela

Alesica Smith

Alesica Smith, an Early Childhood Educator, was raised in Wickliffe, Ohio by her parents along with her two siblings. She raised three of her own children and is now also a grandmother. Alesica has a passion and love for reading, animals, and art. She is a woman of great strength and resilience, with a deep spiritual foundation that underlies everything she does. She is particularly passionate about rescuing and rehabilitating animals in need.

As a writer, Alesica hopes to draw inspiration from her own life experiences. In sharing her writing she wants to candidly explore these themes that offer hope, love, empathy, and gratitude to assist others who may be facing similar challenges.

Despite the difficulties she has faced, Alesica remains a giving and loving person, always striving to make a positive impact on the world around her.

One thing that Alesica always says is: Look for the GOOD!!

GRATITUDE

By Alesica Smith

It's the only way I know how to begin. I go to bed at night with it and wake up to it. There's not one reason for me not to, you see, I'm like a kitty with nine lives over. I've been taken by a chronic illness multiple times and been given my life back. I'm thankful to the skillful paramedics, doctors, nurses, and the many, many hospital staff members for always giving me a fighting chance to live! Most of all I'm grateful to my family for dealing with the constant scary, unforeseen circumstances. Chronic asthma is an illness that can be underestimated and undetected until it's almost too late. My last experience with it was at the end of November 2020. I was thrown into a seizure during a chronic asthma attack (I suffer from them due to an unknown cause). I was admitted to the hospital and seemed to be doing well. I suffered another attack in the hospital and went into cardiac arrest twice. I was put into a medically induced coma and woke up three or four days later.

There have been many other times when I have been revived from this thing that wants to suck the life out of me. It's also not the first time it's put me into a coma or caused a seizure. I am assured that due to this last occurrence, I have become even more diligent in letting go of things that do not matter. I love life and will continue to do so. Just holding on to it a little tighter now. All life is precious. Have you ever noticed how babies, animals, and nature calm you? I urge you to get more of that! I have found that loving life doesn't have a price and loving yourself is not a selfish thing. YOU are your best strength! I give gratitude to those whether they show the smallest or the biggest amount of care. I know that I am meant to be here and I hope that anyone suffering from chronic illness understands that it's okay to put yourself first, and you are worthy of a life that you love! For those of us who look healthy on the outside but don't feel so good on the inside, we don't have to keep that bottled inside, either. I live a quiet, peaceful life and love myself first. People will respect you for having boundaries, and hopefully, they'll begin to see and understand those things in their lives too.

I trust in myself even though I'm not sure of the path that may lie ahead. I do believe in the power of positive thinking, although sometimes that is hard. There have been so many times when I wanted to give up, but then I remember just how much and how hard I've fought just to breathe so I can stay here. I have accepted the fact that my immune system will be forever compromised, and the illnesses that I suffer from are only a portion of my life. I've had to sacrifice some of the things I love and enjoy because of it. What came with that was the realization that sometimes you just need to stop and breathe! Rest! Take time for yourself. When you lose something you also gain something, even if it comes later on down the road. To lose is to gain, so with that said, I have learned that loss is very much a part of life. Often, the people that you love and who have been counting on will leave you. It's already bad enough that you don't want to ever be another person's burden, but you are also fearful of being left behind. You'll find that they have left you with a lot of baggage and heartache. Once you understand that the baggage is discardable, then you can find the gems that they have left for you. I always say that for every person that you meet, take one lesson with you. Every person that comes into your life has a reason to teach you without them even knowing so.

As for heartache, it needs time. All pain needs soothing and healing. Being alone isn't a bad thing and it doesn't have to be. It's a chance to find solace, meaning, and some understanding of the events that have occurred in your life. Being alone is a chance to remember simplicity. Sometimes we need less to have more. That doesn't mean that you can't still love other people and surround yourself with support. Life can be so simple when you find peace, love, and, yes, gratitude within. Some of the things that I enjoy doing that have helped me along the way are meditation, giving self-Reiki care, as well as sending distance Reiki to aid ailing pets, and the sounds of soft music. Have you ever tried to stay awake while listening to lullabies for babies? Ha! Both me and my fur babies love to fall asleep to hush music! Try it! You'll sleep like a baby. Another thing—don't ever forget the childlike you. Be funny, have fun, and laugh! I didn't used to laugh a whole lot. I was always so serious, but not anymore!

I value life so much and no one is hated here. Life is too short for that and yes, I say so even with all my nine lives. No, I know what you're thinking. It doesn't mean to be someone's personal doormat. It simply means, why go low when you can go high and keep going? There's no sense in going in circles with people. Keep what matters and discard the rest. In writing this, looking back on other past traumatic events that have taken place in my life, it is only now that I realize that I have learned the lesson that I was supposed to and that it has come full circle.

Gratitude. It's BIG! See? Having access to the things that matter to you in your life is a skill and keeping them is mastery. There's so much that my past experiences have taught me about what matters, and they have made such a tremendous impact on my life, so it's only forward that I look now. A person can survive so much, and realize it takes little to be happy. You are not meant to stay stagnant or feel stuck. Love and gratitude will move you! Peace will make you so still. You are worthy of whatever it is that you demand from your life! Right now, out here in this world we live in today, we are lacking in the love of self and the love of each other. We are becoming desensitized to the feelings of others. The lack of empathy and compassion can be seen everywhere and nowhere. I try to live a wholesome life and by doing that, I hope that my story touches someone in a way that makes a positive difference in their life.

I am still a work in progress and, as a work in progress, I need to have a thoughtful mind to recognize my own emotions and have empathy for myself. Understand that if you need to cry, then by all means, cry! Because if there is anything else I've learned, holding back tears makes room for a far worse feeling than a release of water. If you are able to have empathy for yourself, then you can have empathy for others. Everything starts with YOU, even when the purpose is unknown. You have a blueprint that is specifically for you and is not made for anybody else. There were times when I would think to myself, *Why was I chosen for this life? What am I supposed to do with it if I can't do the things I love?* I don't ask those kinds of questions anymore. I have learned to build myself from the traumas of my life. I will always believe that I have a long journey ahead and some wonderful things on the horizon. Hitting rock bottom isn't the same for everyone and you may brush close more than once.

I've learned not to be bothered by others' judgment. I'm a deaf person who was formerly hard of hearing. When I was young, it was still a thing to be deaf, dumb, and mute. So, I learned quickly that expectations of me weren't very high. Life is going to happen to you—good things and bad. How you learn to handle those things and navigate through all the twists, turns, highs, and lows of life is up to you. These things that I have come to realize and utilize in my life are the tools that will keep me building along this journey that we call life. I hope these words fill the hearts of many and help to build a path for you that's all your own.

Becky Lynch

Lake County Ohio
County Recorder

https://www.lakecountyohiorecorder.com/

A strong, business-minded woman with responsible and fair-minded intuitions, Becky Lynch was elected Lake County Ohio's 25th County Recorder since the county was formed in 1840. She's been a business owner since 1992, is happily married to Mike Lynch, and has three grown kids, Brian, Dillon, and Kelly. She was re-elected handily in 2020 to continue the improvements achieved in the Recorder Office such as significant savings to the County General Fund of over a million dollars during her time in office. Becky lives in South Mentor. Born in Zanesville, she was the first-born girl to Jim and Elaine Smith and one of seven kids all growing up in smalltown America. She serves on the National Association of Counties Military and Veterans Services Committee and as Executive Member on her Precinct Committee. Becky cherishes her Faith, which guides her every step. She loves family, golfing badly, and governing whole-heartedly!

REACHING YOUR STAR IN A BROKEN DOWN CAR

By Becky Lynch

Reach for the stars. This was the theme of a card I was given for my high school graduation. It was my absolute favorite card. I kept that card for years! It went to college with me and got pinned to the corkboard above my teeny dorm room desk at Kent State. It was read probably a million times in moments when I wanted to get a little inspiration and confidence. But I think mostly, it was the amazing love and care that the words depicted which I felt came directly from my grandma's heart to my heart! Then the sweetest memories would roll in like a gentle wave when I would see her handwritten "Love You" that warmed my heart. I just knew that what was in that card (albeit some American Greetings card producer's words) was meant especially for me!

As one of seven kids, we had great parents who loved each one of us, encouraging our distinct talents and personalities in the best and most complete way that could ever be dreamt of. We were rich in love rather than money. Never knew the meaning of "poor," even amidst the creamed hamburger on toast and cut-out cardboard inserts to extend the wearability of our black and white saddle shoes! Mom was a registered nurse working the 3-11 shift and Dad was a carpenter/masonry contractor working hard 15 hours a day. As the second oldest girl, with the youngest brother born when I was ten, responsibility came early, and organizational skills became "baked in" to my personality. There was never a dull or quiet moment in our house. What a riot thinking about the chaos! Mom and Dad and seven kids was not only a life carved out of faith, hope, and love, but a lesson in survival of the fastest at the dinner table and survival of the fittest to the best seat in the family station wagon! I didn't do well sitting in the back seat facing tailgating cars, but whichever place we landed was an exercise in patience, at least until we arrived at our destination.

Pragmatism and patience are wonderful traits that are either learned through much effort or, in my case, through the several essential skills that were bequeathed unto me.

A hustle and bustle life makes one open to adventure. Not having but a semester of Spanish under my belt, my college roommate and lifetime best friend talked me into attending a student foreign exchange to Mexico. We would study at La Universidad Veracruzana with the supervisory professor and live with a host family for an entire semester. Three months. No English. What a way to learn a new language! And what a way to spend the "Blizzard of '78," only one of the most historical snow events of the century to hit northeast Ohio! It was a tough road from the start, one of those experiences that you wish you could reverse but too late, you're too far into it (not to mention the blizzard shut down airports and roadways so you're stuck and can't go back home even if you tried). So, there you have it, the lessons of patience were kicking in! But, about a month into the trip the walls started closing in and feelings of being trapped in a foreign place were affecting my grades and enthusiasm. The impulse to "flight" was winning out over the motivation to stay and "fight." I was homesick, young, and unappreciative of the moment. I was feeling sorry for myself and wanted to quit. It was raining on my psyche big time, and I just wanted to give up and go home.

That January night, the family's telephone rang. It seemed louder that time, echoing from the second-floor stucco walls and marble-floored alcove. Most of the time it would be for one of our teenage temporary siblings, but this time it was my Aunt Rosie! She was an executive at the telephone company and had the credentials to make international calls (which were not frequent in those times). My Mexican Mama called me to come to the phone and that's when I was given the news that my beloved Pop had died. He was everything to me, I was his favorite granddaughter, and I knew it! I was the apple of his eye, and he was my hero. It was crushing, paralyzing, a terrible nightmare. What now? Convinced that I could get home and to my Pop's funeral I fought against the odds. But the odds were against me and so was Mother Nature. There was no way in the world for me to get home for any reason, even for the funeral of my Poppy. Quicksand was swallowing me, and I was doomed.

The family had a rooftop garden where they kept greens and a few chickens and a pig. I frequently went there to reflect and hide from my problems of the day. After no more tears would fall from my eyes, I climbed the wavy staircase to the roof. I sat there and just prayed. The stars were sterling bright, and the sky was stunning—deep black, my very own supernatural planetarium. It was breathtaking and it seemed that time had simply stopped. But divine intervention weighed in instead. In an instant all the sky was gone, and clouds had covered every star. Get busy! Show's over. You are not a quitter. You never have been, and you won't start now! Message received. The challenge was accepted and thanks to divine intervention and my Pop, I not only finished the full semester, but my grades went from Ds to As!

After college, I went on my merry way to California in pursuit of fame and fortune. The morning was cool, crisp, and sad for my very loving and concerned parents. The strong-headed daughter they had raised was now causing them the distress most parents experience when children exit the nest. Perhaps their tears were simply au-revoir sadness or maybe, just maybe, it was the fearful notion that the 1972 Ford Maverick, for which I paid a whopping $350 cash, would leave me stranded somewhere just far enough away that they would not be able to come rescue me.

Well, of course, that was exactly what happened! While driving down the road listening to the AM radio drop in and out with each booming metropolis that I passed through, my trusty steed conked out just outside of St. Louis. It took a few days to get repaired but as the saying goes, in times of challenge, look for the silver lining. Stranded and waiting, I shopped around a little store where a little wooden plaque lifted my spirits! It's a poem that charged up my wounded ego.

The encouraging words healed my momentary setback and refueled a newfound "get up and go" attitude. The author is Barbara Burrow and the title of her "Maverick-saving" poem is *That Woman is a Success*. In my hour of need, it worked a miracle with me, and that precious little plaque remains among my greatest treasures! I would like to give you all some of its magic.

That Woman is A Success:

Who loves life and lives it to the fullest,
Who has discovered and shared the strengths and talents that are uniquely
*   her own,*
Who puts her best into each task and leaves each situation better than she
*   found it,*
Who seeks and finds that which is beautiful in all people and all things,
Whose heart is full of love and warm with compassion,
Who has found joy in living and peace within herself.

It was evident early on that there is a long line of strong, independent women in my family, on both sides, and I married into another entire line of the same! It's pretty obvious when the initial meet and greets are slow and steady but at the same time studied and suspicious. It's funny when you get the instant feeling that you are looking in a mirror! After being duly dissected, trust and love have exponentially multiplied over the years. The miracle of family is one of my greatest blessings, with three kids who are all grown and a loving man who still sees me as I was in my twenties—not going to complain about that!

The pragmatic personality pill that I inherited for life's roller coaster came from Mom. She got it from her mom (my "reach for the stars" grandma). It was also passed to my angel on earth sister (who got a little less than my dose because she's a middle child). And I passed it to my amazing daughter who is soon to be a registered nurse, following in the footsteps of my mom, who spent her legendary life healing and helping our fellow humans as a registered nurse as well. Confidently we, endowed with "strong and mighty," go along day by day dropping little pieces of pragmatism around the planet. If one can get jazzed up about the thought of pragmatic positivity—which is synonymic with the diplomacy of realism, reasonableness, rationality, practicality, and logic—then once in a while, we may find ourselves effortlessly smiling at each other, giving a compassionate look or a pat on the back to another and making it easier for those we encounter to also "reach for the stars."

Chrissty Tryon

Ohio State Bar Association Certified Paralegal

https://www.linkedin.com/in/chrissty-tryon-a7b82629b/
https://www.facebook.com/chrissty.tryon

I received my Paralegal Studies Associate Degree from Kent State University in 2006. I am an Ohio State Bar Association Certified Paralegal. I am an active member of the Ohio State Bar Association and the National Association of Legal Assistants (NALA). I am working toward an Advanced Certified Paralegal Credential from NALA.

I was previously employed as a paralegal with The Iarocci Law Firm for nine years working on estates, estate planning, personal injury, family law, and corporate law. I was also employed with the Ashtabula County Prosecutor's office as a paralegal working in the felony and civil offices before moving into a human resources and office manager position. While there I also was a super user for the Matrix Prosecutor and Matrix Civil case management systems and trained employees on this system.

I live in Andover, Ohio with my husband and son and fur children.

ENJOY THE JOURNEY

By Chrissty Tryon

I am the oldest child of Ronnie and Nancy (Fanyon) Cline and have been a lifelong Ohio resident. I was an average student and was never forced to really apply myself. I was involved in Teen Institute, Year Video, and school and church choirs. I graduated from Berkshire High School in Burton, Ohio in 1993. I attended Kent State University after graduation but was uncertain about my path of study so I took a break from college after the first year. I worked as a bank teller and telecommunications analyst.

I returned to college in 2002 to complete an associate's degree in paralegal studies while working full-time. This was a really big decision for me as neither of my parents had gone to college, nor had my sister. At that time, I was employed as a secretary at Warren and Young PLL in Ashtabula, Ohio, and completed an internship in estates and estate planning under the direction of Theresa Watson and Stuart Cordell, Esq. I was also awarded a scholarship from PEO (Philanthropic Educational Organization) Sisterhood to help pay for my education while working full-time. Working at Warren and Young PLL was foundational in my career as I was exposed to different areas of law and learned additional office skills.

In my last semester of college, I was taking a class at Lakeland Community College and working full-time. On my way home from school in early November I hit a deer with my car. It was late at night, dark, and that deer seemed to come out of nowhere. The next day I was pretty sore and went to see my doctor who wanted to get X-rays of my neck and back. My husband, Tom, and I had been dealing with infertility and although it seemed unlikely at the time that I could be pregnant, the doctor still had to test me prior to X-rays. I will never forget when the doctor came into the room and said, "Guess what?"

and handed me the positive test. What a mix of emotions. Tom and I had been married for years at that point. I had just lost my dad in May and was getting ready to graduate college. I graduated from Kent State University in December 2006 with an associate's degree in paralegal studies. We shared the news of the pregnancy with our families on New Year's Day 2007.

We were in for a long road of difficulties. From the start, the numbers and labs came back with issues. I was considered a high-risk pregnancy and the doctors wanted to take an amniocentesis. By the numbers, there was a chance that our child would have a birth defect. We declined the procedure. This child was our gift from above and we were prepared to deal with any birth defect that may come. I had frequent medical appointments and ultrasounds and, in addition to my regular obstetrician, I also saw a specialist for high-risk patients and had a book of ultrasound pictures. My husband attended all the ultrasounds with me except the last one. We had agreed that we would not find out the sex and even painted the baby's room yellow. Most of the family thought that we were having a girl, but I did not think so. The last ultrasound I had to attend alone, and it was my opportunity to find out the sex. We were having a boy. I kept that to myself until delivery time.

Many women like to be pregnant, but I have to say I hated every minute of it. I recall going to church and saying, "This kid can come anytime." That Thursday, I woke up with incredible pain and bleeding and this went on for a couple of hours before calling the doctor. The doctor very calmly said he would meet us at the hospital. We arrived at the hospital at 3:00 a.m. We didn't know our way around and things were very uncertain. When we arrived at the maternity floor everyone seemed to know what was going on, but we didn't. I was having a placenta abruption and things progressed very rapidly. At 9:01 a.m. Zachary Andrew Tryon was born eight weeks premature. We never heard him cry and he was a pale shade of blue-purple. He was quickly taken away and there was an army of nurses and staff working on him. We would later learn that Zachary had to be resuscitated and that he had underdeveloped lungs due to being born prematurely. He was born at St. Joseph Warren Hospital where they didn't have a NICU.

After about an hour I got to hold him for a few moments, and a nurse took a Polaroid picture before he was taken by ambulance to St. Elizabeth's Hospital in Boardman. There I was, left with a Polaroid picture and unable to hold my newborn. This was when found my voice. I was to advocate for this four-pound little boy that I had waited so long for. Zachary spent 23 days in the NICU before being discharged on an apnea monitor on May 19, 2007—one year to the day that I lost my dad. That had to be a God-wink. Zachary would be in quarantine until December 2007, only being permitted to go to medical appointments. One of the worst sounds a parent can hear is the apnea monitor alarm. That meant that he had stopped breathing, or that his heart had stopped. Tom and I were trained in pediatric CPR and how to operate the apnea monitor. I have had to continue to fight with insurance, doctors, and teachers to this day. Zachary was later diagnosed with learning disabilities and autism.

In 2008 my health started to decline. Doctors suggested that any further pregnancies would be life-threatening for me, which was devastating. I never wanted Zachary to be an only child and really wanted him to have a brother. Things would get progressively worse over the next several years and I would have several surgeries for endometriosis. I would never fully recover after surgery but always returned to work. At my worst, I would drag myself to work and then come home and go to bed. I was going to physical therapy and the therapist told me about a functional medicine clinic downtown. I was interested and called the next day, making an appointment for the next week. Another God-wink moment: I was supposed to be there. There was a typical wait time of four months for new patients. Once at the appointment, I had the most thorough exam I have ever had. I had previously been diagnosed with autoimmune diseases; this doctor suspected that I had Lyme disease. Most Lyme disease testing and treatments are not covered by insurance and are out-of-pocket. I waited to be tested because the test was going to be near $2,000. The test came back positive for Lyme and co-infections of Lyme. Lyme is a peculiar thing because it can mimic other conditions. I have been on a long road of antibiotics, supplements, dietary changes, and therapies with minimal relief.

I started my small business called *My Fleece Works* in October 2020. My business name comes from a Bible verse in Proverbs 31:13—"She seeks wool and flax and works with her hands." I have had chronic illness for years and am not always able to participate in outings with my family. I had to find something I could do on my own when I was stuck at home. I also found that being wrapped up in a warm fleece blanket or two with my fur babies was comforting. By the time I decided on entrepreneurship, all my friends and family had already been gifted a fleece blanket, so what was I to do with the remainder of my inventory? I realized I could use this as an avenue to spread awareness of Lyme disease.

I learned many lessons from these life events:

1. Know that God is always with you, even when it doesn't seem things are going right. Chronic illness is lonely and people often don't know what you are going through. I tell my husband all the time I should put a sign on my back with all my diagnoses. Yes, I'm in pain.
2. Don't rely on others for your happiness.
3. Believe in yourself. I learned that I am my own worst enemy and the only one holding me back is me.
4. Life is precious and to be valued. Losing my dad was devastating for me and we nearly lost Zachary. Value the time you have with your loved ones.

Christina Mott

Paralegal

https://www.facebook.com/Christina.Mott1470
https://www.instagram.com/Cmott3/

My name is Christina Mott. I am currently a paralegal for a small local firm. I earned my paralegal certification through the University of Akron, and my Victim Advocacy certification through NOVA.

I am currently the 2023 Mrs. Ohio AmeriFest, where my platform includes victim and veteran advocacy. I enjoy being able to help others overcome shyness, set goals, build healthy habits, character, sportsmanship, self discipline, and confidence as they help me do the same.

During the day I enjoy music, photography, and homesteading in the city. I love teaching my children skills from our great grandparents and having my own little farm in the city.

STILL STANDING

By Christina Mott

If everything worked out the way you thought you wanted it to, imagine what you'd be missing out on today…This is my motto for my life. I used to wonder where I would be if I had had a decent childhood, but now I sit and think about how lucky I am for those trials and tribulations. They made me the person I am today and the person I am no longer.

Childhood trauma is hard, and it's hard to break the cycle. I love my mother and the sacrifices she made for our family. Like many, she had her own problems, and, looking back at things now, I realize that she wasn't really in a healthy place to have children at the time. As a result, my brother and I were often abused, both mentally and physically. Growing up, children often said, "Sticks and stones will break my bones but words will never hurt me." As a survivor, I can say wholeheartedly that words absolutely do hurt others, and those wounds don't always heal.

I remember my mother had a tendency to meet random men online, which led to even more problems for our family. When I was around the age of 12, she met a man who claimed to be a Christian. We went to visit him. After a short stay, we returned home and I told my mother I didn't want to move there with him. Like times before, she disregarded my concerns and protests, moved us in with him, and, soon after, married him.

Everything changed for me after that. This "Christian" man had my mother sleep on the couch while his biological daughter and I were forced to stay in his bed with him. He would often say out loud, "Your daughter is a better wife than you." My mother would walk into the room where we were being molested without saying a word, putting up a fight, or trying to protect me.

Eventually, we moved back to Ohio. My brother was placed in the custody of the state, while I permanently lived with my grandmother who had her hands full after already raising her own children.

In high school, I turned to self-harm as a relief to escape the memories of my past. I was a good student, so no one suspected that anything was wrong or that I was struggling so badly. Eventually, my best friend told an officer at school, which led to the first steps of getting help.

I remember sitting in my therapist's office, looking at the floor. We'd discovered that I was more likely to open up when I wasn't looking at her. It felt less vulnerable. And for the first time in more than a decade of therapy, I started to talk about feelings I'd never shared. I told her that for my entire life, I'd had a sense that I was being taken advantage of. Then, out of nowhere, I said, "Even when I'm allowing it." It was my moment of clarity which I always thought was a weakness...I finally realized I wasn't at fault, I was a child and my childhood had been taken from me. My counselor was amazing and was the reason I made the decision to report the abuse that had happened in my childhood. It was a long journey that involved 10 years of outpatient counseling and two in-patient hospital stays. We ended up charging my stepdad for the abuse he inflicted on us. Ultimately my mother was not able to testify because she would be "testifying against herself." I remember being asked if I was okay with that, and I knew I had to keep other children safe from him as well, so although it took six years, the jury finally decided to convict this monster and sentenced him to 109 years for his abuse.

Watching the case unfold, the trauma that was re-inflicted, and the inner workings of the criminal justice system would bring me to the point of wanting to become a paralegal. This dream is rooted in my desire to actively work in victim advocacy so I can help others who may need the support and experience of someone who understands. I was lucky enough to have strong people who stayed by my side through the years-long journey of reliving the torture and shame that I felt. Others deserve the same.

I am now the mother to three great children, something I always thought was taken from me. I had always doubted that I could break the cycle and give my children a life I didn't have. I did that, they have no knowledge of the life I had before them, and I work hard and diligently to make sure they never will. I now work part-time at a local firm. It's not easy, and I'm so thankful for those who stood by my side and held me accountable. Because of them, I was able to prove that statistics are just a number, and they do not define you.

Courtney Smith

I am only 27 and was once a preschool teacher for 8 years before I realized I was miserable and could just quit. Just like I was once abused, I realized I could just leave. I am now in a healthy, long-term relationship and am a cat mom. I am currently working toward owning a homestead with my partner and being employed by no one. I have two older brothers and awesome parents who are still married after almost 40 years. Sometimes, even with a great upbringing, you just choose the wrong path. Remember, you are the creator of your environment. You are allowed to just leave, or just quit. Thank you for taking interest in my life and I hope this has helped you in some way.

THE GREAT ESCAPE

By Courtney Smith

Let me start off by saying that it could have been much worse. Many other women have suffered longer than I did and have lived through more frightening events. I do not compare myself to them, nor do I put my trauma above theirs. My story is not unique, but I do look back on this time as an experience I feel lucky to have had. I came out alive and I learned a lot about myself, who I was, and who I wanted to be. But I also learned about boundaries, expectations, and love. This is when I started to become the best version of myself, and I am eternally grateful for that.

Everyone asked me, "If it was that bad, why'd you stay?" Well, I'll tell you half the answer now: because it wasn't always bad. I thought he was a great person and we had a lot of fun together in the beginning. He was outgoing, adventurous, respectful. He came from a good family and he treated me well. I truly did love him. And that says a lot about the person I was at the time. I never thought it would happen to me, and I loved with rose-colored glasses.

He started out small, becoming upset at things I found to be silly. I would cave, apologize for causing him distress, and we'd move on. No big deal, right? For me, it wasn't! I was a very codependent person and thought it was normal for people to become easily upset with me and that it was my responsibility to make it right. I'm sure he realized this instantly and that's why he kept me around. It would escalate slowly, making me feel bad for his sad life. He had that "everything that happens to me is someone else's fault" type of attitude. And I fell for it.

It turned into screaming matches, where he would put me down and I would be so sorry for being stupid. Because not conforming to what others expect you to be is something to be ashamed of, right? A perfect example of this would be his birthday. He had been working a job out of town, being home only two or three days a week. He was not planning to be home on his actual birthday, so I gave him his gift a week early (a brand-new acoustic guitar). He ended up coming home on his birthday at the last minute, so we spent the day together. His mom made him a nice dinner and we went out shopping. While we were out, he started making comments about how I didn't "plan anything" for him. I reminded him that I'd had no idea he would be home until that day. He mentioned that every year, someone always throws some type of party or get-together for him on his birthday and nobody did that this year. I tried making him feel better, telling him we could do something with friends the next day, but he wasn't having it. He was now having the textbook definition of a "temper tantrum." He begins throwing all the blame on me, saying, "I don't even want you to come home tonight! You can stay at your mom's!" I was shaken. Why? No clue! I should have known that he would actually pull into my parents' house five minutes later and say, "Get out." The only thing I regret about that night is not leaving the car door open so that he would be forced to get out himself and shut it. But don't worry, I apologized for my "actions" the next day after my dad drove me home.

Let's talk about sexual abuse. Fair warning, this will be triggering. All of the abuse I endured was not recognizable as abuse to me, rape included. I know, how is that even possible? It's like this: Imagine waking up in the middle of the night to find your partner already inside you. Did he try to wake you up before? Did you consent in your sleep? The first time it happened to me, I assumed the answer was yes and just…continued. We never spoke about it, mostly because I didn't want to have that conversation. I just wanted to forget it and move on. My memory only recalls this happening one other time, with the addition of being tied up. I awoke to find my feet roped together at the end of the bed and my hands restrained behind my back. I was lying on my stomach and he, again, was already inside me. This is when I realized I wasn't crazy, that it wasn't just me making a big deal out of nothing. But still, I suffered through it and carried on until it was over. I was the perfect candidate for rape.

I have a feeling that this happened more than these two times and I am just suppressing the memory. It's very hard for anyone to conceptualize their partner, with whom they've already been sexually active, raping them. Other forms of sexual abuse include (but are not limited to) taking suggestive photographs of you without your consent, pressuring you to watch pornography or sleep with their friends, or selling your body for money.

This is my first time opening up about my sexual abuse. I never even told my therapist. However, I am saying it now despite my embarrassment and dignity, in hopes of reaching the right person and showing the world that this is not normal, nor appropriate, behavior for your partner to be displaying.

In between all of this, he was slowly pulling me away from my friends and family. I didn't even realize it until it was almost too late. I let important friendships fall through the cracks and it was always awkward to be around my family. These are things I know I took for granted and absolutely allowed to happen. It was just so quick that I never had time to stop and think about how it happened. I don't take full credit for what I went through, but it does take two.

So, how did I make my great escape? I waited until he became physical. Not intentionally, but that's what happened. He was having another episode, furious about the dinner I had cooked for him. He took his plate full of food, chucked it, and broke the window. He went to the kitchen and began throwing pots and pans at me. I cautiously kept my phone nearby so if I needed to call the police, I could. But he was on me like a hawk. There was more throwing, pushing me against the wall, spitting in my face, and yet, he still made me pick up the broken glass from the window, board it up, and clean all the food. I understood then that I was a slave.

I was scared to sleep next to him that night, but I knew he wouldn't have it any other way. He started telling me that I should call off work the next day, hell, even quit my job! But I couldn't let that happen, work was my escape. So, I got up the next morning while he was still asleep, secretly packed a bag, and headed off to work telling him I would see him later.

I never came back.

So, "If it was that bad, why'd you stay?" Here's the rest of the answer: because staying is easier. Staying means he won't come looking for me, that there's no chance to set him off more, that maybe I can make this better. Leaving requires guts, and if you're already this deep into the relationship, you have none. But once I freed myself, I could do anything! Don't get me wrong, the weeks to come were just as traumatic. Trips to the police station, court, fear of seeing him in every public place I went to. But it was worth it. RIP to that girl!

I used to think to myself, "If I had just known the signs. If I just had more confidence. If I had just cooked something else." But then I realized that I could choose a different mindset. I can choose to learn the lesson and move on. I can choose any path I want and make my own decisions. This is such a small lesson, but one that I didn't learn until I was grown. Now that I have this mentality, I am choosing to love me.

It's important to understand that when I say this version of me is dead, I mean, quite literally, she does not exist. We may have the same eye color, hair color, and passion for tacos and caffeine. But she did not go to the gym, cook her own meals, have any tattoos, or stand up for herself. I can't even wear the clothes I used to own! I would put them on, look in the mirror, and feel nothing but discomfort. I've diagnosed myself with mild body dysmorphia. Regardless, I became my own bodyguard, physically and mentally, and it was the best decision I ever made.

Crystal Welsh

https://www.linkedin.com/in/crystal-kathleen-welsh-69025957
https://www.facebook.com/crystal.welsh.9/
https://www.instagram.com/crystal.welsh.12/

Since graduating from her undergraduate education, Crystal has held a variety of roles in her 18-plus year career. From social services to legal services to prosecutorial roles, Crystal approaches each challenge with an analytical lens and a desire to make a difference.

Crystal is a funny, compassionate, and educated woman. She loves her family, dogs, and of course, "her peeps." While she is not normally comfortable sharing details about her life with the world, she was asked to highlight her journey in life and touch on the things that have impacted her the most. She hopes that was done here and feels it was an honor to be included.

THE VOICE WITHIN

By Crystal Welsh

I worked hard to achieve everything I have in life. I started working when I was fifteen years old and was excited to buy my first car. I remember it being a rusted-out Chevy Cavalier, one you had to throw in neutral and rev the engine just to prevent it from stalling at red lights. However, it was a fantastic car, as it was all mine.

There was never any doubt that college was the next step after high school. There was always a voice inside my head telling me that's what was next, even though I was the first person in my immediate family to go to college. I had to take out student loans, which ultimately made me appreciate my education more. I knew what it was costing me and what sacrifices it was taking me to get what I wanted. I worked three jobs while attending Cleveland State University for my undergraduate education and achieved my bachelor's degree in sociology with a concentration in criminology. I worked at Build-A-Bear Workshop, Kay Jewelers, and the third shift at a Speedway gas station. I still remember crossing the street in the mornings thinking how I could easily take a nap on the cement and how the curb would make a nice pillow. I was exhausted most days. I also babysat from the time I was 15 through the early years of college. There were certainly fun times, especially since I was living with my brother off-campus; however, I worked hard and struggled to get to graduation day. During my time in college, I met my soon-to-be husband and dealt with all the dynamics that married life entails.

Once I graduated from Cleveland State University, summa cum laude, I landed in public service. I was a social worker in the Children Services division of the Lake County Department of Job and Family Services for almost ten years. During that time, I worked with families on an ongoing basis to try to keep them together. Unfortunately, that didn't always happen, and I sometimes had to remove children from their homes—at times, permanently. There were positive stories, such as the children who were able to be adopted by their forever families when their biological families were unable to support them. Unfortunately, there were also tales of sadness that broke my heart. I recall one time when I had to pick up a foster kid from the police station because his mother got arrested for shoplifting, despite being on thin ice already. Nobody safe was able to take him and he was forced to go back into the system. I still remember his mother crying, him getting teary-eyed, and having to tell him to hug her goodbye and that we were going to go for a ride together to my friend's house for him to spend some time with them. Thankfully he knew me, and thankfully he came to me—it could have been a lot harder. A harder time was taking a baby from the hospital the day after she was born right from her mother's room. Those memories still stay with me. There are many stories.

After years as a social worker, I decided that my calling was actually in the legal field, where I felt I could do more for the community. I embarked on my legal education and was accepted to Cleveland Marshall College of Law. I continued to work as a social worker while attending night classes. This extended my schooling to four years as opposed to three. I still remember taking tax law until ten o'clock at night, walking to my car, being not only exhausted but confused and questioning some of my life choices. I still found time to enjoy life and took my family on a couple of cruises. You can't get time back, and I tried to appreciate every moment that I could. On a positive note, during this time I was able to work to pay off my undergraduate student loans. However, I was only accumulating additional, significantly higher loans for my juris doctorate. Also during this time, I dealt with medical issues with two family members. First, unforeseen and unknown to me, my uncle was battling cancer. I can recall how one of his children chose not to attend family Christmas so as not to reveal the sad truth that we were all soon to have to face. I didn't understand the full extent until later, when another medical issue reared its ugly head, this time hitting closer to home. Losing a parent is like being in a private club; no one knows what it's like until you are in it and unfortunately it's a dreadful club that nobody wants to be a part of.

After four long years in law school, I finally graduated cum laude. It was hard not having my mother be a part of that success. With over $100,000 in debt and no job prospects to speak of it was a little daunting and overwhelming. However, I had a husband to lean on which made it more bearable. In order to pay off my educational loans, I stumbled into donating plasma. It helped to relieve some of the financial strain on the life of a new marriage and a struggling recent law school graduate.

Eventually, I found a job in the private sector which at least enabled me to make money; however, it was not my passion. I wanted to use my education to truly make a difference in the community. I was ready to throw away my law degree because I was frustrated that I could not find a job as a prosecutor, as that was the work I felt was my calling. Then, an adjunct professor I had during law school allowed me to interview at her firm for a social worker position, as I had that educational background. However, she created an additional attorney role specifically for me. I joined her firm and discovered a newfound passion for the law. During my time at her firm, the Lake County Prosecutor's Office contacted me to join their office. I weighed the pros and cons but ultimately accepted, as it was my dream job. I was very happy to be working there and was ultimately promoted to supervisor of the juvenile division after only a year of employment, allowing me to oversee approximately seven staff attorneys.

Ultimately life took me away from Lake County to Bellefontaine, Ohio, as the City Prosecutor. I worked diligently during my three years in Bellefontaine, and I got to know and love the community. Looking for new challenges, I decided to run for Municipal Court Judge. During my run for Judge, I spent countless hours attending township meetings, posting signs, crafting mailers, getting to know the community members, and attending party meetings and other social events, all funded from a civil servant's paycheck. Despite my efforts and hard work, I lost the election. While it was initially very heartbreaking, I still learned and gained friends and experiences that will last a lifetime.

I remain as the city prosecutor for the Bellefontaine community and I continue to feel supported by this town I now call home. I have met many law enforcement professionals who rely on me and continue to contact me for support and guidance. Just as my career experienced changes, a lot of people came and went in my life, unfortunately including my husband. However, they all taught me a lesson and made me who I am today. I am grateful for everyone who has made an impact on my life.

Looking back over my life, there were many opportunities where I could have decided to quit. Those long nights working the third shift, the crippling weight of student loan debt, the loss of my mother, the ending of my marriage, the unsuccessful run for judge, and others. However, something in me would not let me quit. The encouragement of friends, family, and colleagues certainly played a role, but I also think I owe it to the voice within that told me to just keep going, despite setbacks. I do not regret any choices I made or the directions my life took me. Everything is a learning experience and made me who I am today. It has not always been an easy road; I have had many struggles along the way, but I would encourage anyone experiencing setbacks to listen to that voice within. At the end of the day, the only one we truly have to make proud is ourselves, and the only expectations we have to meet are our own.

Darcy Bartlett

Hi, I'm Darcy and I am an alcoholic. I'm also a mother of two and a grandmother of two, a daughter, a sister, and aunt, a niece, a best friend, and a sponsor in AA. I would not have any of this if not for the divine intervention that occurred on December 17, 2019—the day that would change the rest of my life. I am so very blessed to be retired so I can do the things God intended, one of which is helping others who also suffer from the very cunning, baffling, powerful disease of addiction, by sharing myself and my story, which in turn helps me stay clean and sober, and become a better everything. The media completely destroyed my character. With the help of my loving God, and the eventual support of my awesome, loving family, I can now hold my head up higher than it's ever been.

IT AIN'T EASY BEING GREEN

By Darcy Bartlett

My older sister gave me a tiny little book with that sentence on the cover the first time I drove myself to in-patient care at Glenbeigh hospitals in Rock Creek, Ohio, about 15 years ago. I was released after (only) 16 days because my insurance said so. My counselors said I was ready, my doctors there said I was ready, Glenbeigh in general said I was ready. Little did they know…

I may have been ready as far as alcohol and drugs were concerned, but as far as my mental, emotional, and spiritual health? Not even close. You see, AA, NA, Glenbeigh, etc…they teach you how to stay clean and sober, they give you the proper tools to use, and they're always there for you when and if you reach out. For me personally, it has taken two trips to Glenbeigh, being arrested, going to jail, being in the newspaper and on national TV, and being charged with a Class 4 Felony to realize I needed way more than that!

My mother was pregnant with me (the baby of the three) when she caught my dad with the 16-year-old babysitter. They divorced, she remarried him again, caught them again, and divorced when I was two. Not to brag but I was the cutest little towhead—wearing homemade dresses from grandma—that you've ever seen. How could he just leave?! Not to mention leaving my five-and-a-half-year-old brother and my 10-year-old sister. What kind of man does that? He wasn't a man if you ask me. Here come the issues:

1. Abandonment
2. Not being good enough (a major one)
3. Never knowing the love of a man

The proof is in the pudding. Just check out my track record to this day.

I've been single for almost four years now, the longest I've been single since 6th grade. I was then taken to my grandma's and great-grandma's house on the lake at the Hallwood Beach community. My aunt and uncle lived right next door. But everyone worked (my mom had three jobs) except me and Bapchi (great-grandma in Polish), who spoke only Polish, so from 2-5 years old this is where I spent my days. I also spent my Saturday nights there watching Lawrence Welk, eating windmill cookies, and drinking hot tea so Grandma Mary could take me to St. Pete's for church. At the age of seven, my life as I knew it would no longer be. We were introduced to a man named John Frey, who soon became our "stepdad" and my mom's second husband.

I'm not going to go into a lot of detail; John was an alcoholic. I can't remember exactly when the abuse started; all I know is that it did. If I think about it (which I try not to), I can still hear my tiny little mom screaming his name to stop. I hated that man with every ounce of my being.

We moved to the "city," W. 19th, aka Carpenter, right nextdoor to a little set of projects. We went from a solitary farmhouse on Brooks Road to actually having neighbors! Let the fun begin. I started drinking to get drunk at age 13. I went to school just to play sports. I was always pretty happy-go-lucky; no one had a clue what was going on behind closed doors at my so-called home.

There were times at this house when I had to hide my mom from John. He would pull in and I would hurry and hide her in the garage, then when he went into the house, I'd take her to our next door neighbors. Sometimes I would have to take my half-sister (yes, John was her dad), 10 years younger than me, up to the attic with books or music, and shut the door so she wouldn't have to hear the awful things I heard when I was little and still had to hear. Whether she heard or not, I can't remember. The following years included:

1. Going into Freshman year, my mom packed me and my little sister up in the middle of the night and drove us to Florida. We moved in with my aunt and uncle. My uncle used to come to me at bedtime with wine.

2. I came home to my aunt's one day from County Side High School to find John and my mother lying on the couch together, him rubbing her back. Needless to say, after three months, we moved back to Ashtabula. My older siblings were out on their own by this time, both in college.

3. Abuse slowed down. John went to Glenbeigh at some point. John was then a detective at the Sheriff's Department. He drove his convertible Corvette around Jefferson fairgrounds at high speed, crashed, and almost killed the woman in the passenger's seat; thank God it wasn't my mother. They finally divorced.

4. I graduated. Between then and the age of 23, I lived in five different states.

5. I had my first and only beautiful daughter at 23 and married her dad six months later.

6. Four years later I had my son. I loved my kids more than anything in the world. Drinking and hard drugs were in and out of most of my adult life.

7. I divorced the kids' dad when I found out he was smoking crack instead of taking care of his kids. I worked nights bartending, the perfect occupation for an alcoholic.

My employment during this time included working as a dental assistant in North Carolina, driving a school bus, working as a bartender for over 10 years, a construction worker, a dump truck driver, and finally getting hired at the post office in 1998.

I was a very functional alcoholic and drug addict. I raised my kids alone. I sometimes worked seven days a week, 10-12 hours a day, and worked holidays including Christmas for the first nine years of my career as a letter carrier. After, I became a regular and had the same route every day in a not-so-decent neighborhood. That was when my addiction was saying, "Oh yeah, this is where we need to be." Being a regular allowed me to get to know people more. I became friends with a lot of them and could get basically anything I wanted. Pills were my drug of choice then, due to my first knee surgery. The prescription ended and the doctor wouldn't give me any more, so I turned to the streets. I liked Percocet and I liked to snort it. It gave me energy. At the end of that phase, at $30 a pill and taking two or three a day, I quit cold turkey. I took a week off of work and slept all week and that was the end of my pill addiction.

In November of 2007, before the pills, I drove myself to Glenbeigh for a cocaine addiction. On March 13, 2009, my "dad" passed away from throat cancer. Being clean and sober but without the support of a program, I had nothing to protect me from my disease. I then proceeded to have a 15-year relapse. I was in and out of AA for many years until December 17, 2019. The consequences of my addiction include:

1. Pushing both of my adult children away.
2. Almost killing myself flipping a 4-wheeler on top of myself without a helmet.
3. Losing a house I had purchased and re-done—it was foreclosed on.
4. My son almost didn't graduate high school. He had missed almost two years, due to the inflammation of H-Pylori, which caused him to vomit alot. All of that due to nerves and anxiety over me going to treatment.
5. Losing two good men who loved me, because of my abusive drinking.
6. Almost getting killed riding my horse around Jefferson Fairgrounds track, drunk out of my mind. My foot got caught

in the stirrup and my horse dragged me around the track unconscious. My left hamstring was torn from the bone. I was in a plastic cast from my ankle to my chest for three months. The inside of my right thigh muscle is crushed from the horse stepping on it.

7. I was evicted from a house I was renting, still in Jefferson. I couldn't work and had zero sick time, so I lost that place too.

I moved back to Ashtabula, went back to work, and everything was right with the world. I was still drinking, though. I met a guy who everyone warned me about on my new route, who later led me to what I now know as the devil—crack cocaine!

The consequences of that were:

1. I lost thousands and thousands of dollars.
2. I would let him take my car (with no driver's license), give him money, and then wouldn't see him for days.
3. I had a car "stolen" and had two cars impounded multiple times.
4. I missed a lot of work and was fired for six months. I got my job back with a pretty nice chunk of backpay only to use that all up drinking and drugging—$26,000!
5. I had a storage space in Saybrook where I kept my mountain bike, camping equipment, and very special things of my grandma's that were passed down to me. Lots of irreplaceable things were auctioned off because he said he would pay the monthly rent on it and did not.
6. Money and items from my house were stolen.
7. I was knocked down and pinned to the ground with a knife at my throat.

I felt justified in smoking crack because I wasn't drinking. That's how sick this disease of addiction and alcoholism really is.

This kind of life went on until December 17, 2019, the day I was arrested at the air pump at Circle K, two blocks from my house. I looked in my rear-view mirror, and I was surrounded by undercover officers, deputies, city police, a postal inspector, and two out-of-state undercovers. I looked up to God and said, "Thank you." I knew the rat race was over.

All of the lying and deceiving. All of the poor choices and decisions. All of the borrowing money, chasing the drugs all day every day. I wasn't sure what was in store for me; all I knew was my shoulders felt 1,000 pounds lighter.

I went to jail for the first time in my life. It was the best experience, and it was exactly what I needed. The girls on the pod were the best—first belly laugh I'd had in months. I wish I could say it was the same for my family. They didn't know what had happened to me until they saw it on the news. Supposedly it was on the news nationwide and in the local papers. I have not read or watched anything about it to this day. From what I heard from friends and family, most of it was lies! Cops went to my son and told lies, Channel 19 news told lies, the Star Beacon told lies! I was asked to resign from the post office. God bless whoever it was who decided not to press charges and let me retire. I'd be in prison right now if that hadn't been the case. And I owe the world to my lawyer (a family friend), who worked his magic as well. I was released on December 24, Christmas Eve. I walked down the main street in Jefferson, where my kids live, with my postal uniform on. Talk about the walk of shame. My lawyer gave me a ride home, to my home that was raided, completely torn upside down only to find nothing. They found nothing because I wasn't the dealer they made me out to be. The guy they really wanted was staying in my spare room, but they couldn't get him. He left my house the night before my arrest with all his stuff so they settled for me, which would make a better story I'm guessing; stories are exactly what they were.

I was charged with a fourth degree felony. No more jail time and two years of probation.

My family, my kids mainly, did not want anything to do with me for a year and a half after the arrest.

A good friend of mine employed at Glenbeigh said they had an open bed available, and I said I'd take it. I had permission from the CEO at the time to continue going to Glenbeigh for as long as it took. Outpatient of course. I said I was going to continue going there until they hired me. I've always felt safe there. God had other plans. COVID hit that March, and I was no longer able to go to Glenbeigh. No outside people.

I continued on like I always do. I asked one of the best sponsors around to be my sponsor. I had a couple of slip-ups, but I am slowly and confidently finding my place in this thing we call life. God has never given up on me. He has always done for me what I couldn't or wouldn't do for myself. He's put a lot of work into me, so I know he's not done yet.

I'm currently back together with my whole family. I get to see my grandkids anytime I want. I've been fighting Social Security Disability for three years now. Time to get another lawyer, I think. I'm trying to start my own business, Serenity Succulents. This is the longest I've been single my whole adult life. I can now be alone and be okay. What a great feeling. I'm still very much a work in progress.

I do have a story to tell, and this is just a fraction of it. I know now that I was chosen to help others with the disease of addiction. I'm hoping to be able to someday help kids who are growing up in an abusive household, or abused women. I am the sponsor to a couple of ladies in AA. There is nothing better than seeing the light and the beauty come to life in the eyes of someone who has been living in the darkness of drugs and alcohol for way too long. That includes the person looking back at me in the mirror.

Darlene Sharpe

University Hospitals
RN

My name is Darlene. I have been happily married for thirty years to my best friend. We have six children between us. Yours, mine, and ours. We also have ten grandchildren and two dogs, a dachshund and a sheep dog. Our children are spread all over the country: Alaska, Oklahoma, Florida, North Carolina, and Ohio. Two served in the Navy and two in the Air force.

I have worked in the medical field my entire life, in nursing homes as an aid, sterile processing in a hospital, in a physician's office as a medical assistant. I was also the medical supervisor at an assisted living facility and now am finally an RN in a hospital. I enjoy helping others and love that I am able to do this and get paid. It has been a long road to get where I am today but I would not change a thing.

NEVER GIVE UP

By Darlene Sharpe

I started nursing school in my early 20s. There were so many things going on in my life at that time that I needed to drop out. I lost my father and my grandfather, and then my mother started having some issues. I had to put my dreams on the back burner at that time. Life then caught up with me. I started a family, I was working, and I just did not have time to return to school. This is the way I thought it was supposed to be, and I continued down that path for many years.

When my youngest daughter decided in her senior year that she was joining the Navy, I decided to re-enroll in college to pursue my nursing degree. This was a very difficult decision for me to make; I had been out of school for so many years at this point, and I was in my late 40s. I have to say, I was terrified at the reality of going back. The thought of writing papers, taking tests, and most likely being one of the oldest students in my class felt so overwhelming, but I put one foot in front of the other and applied. I started with all my prerequisites. Taking classes again after being out of school for many years was very difficult. Writing papers again, and even figuring out how to APA format a paper, was a daunting task.

I do feel that being older and really wanting to accomplish my dream made me a better student, however, because if I did not know how to do something I would find a way to learn how. It may have taken me hours to write a paper that another student spent thirty minutes on, but it was my paper and I was proud of it. I will say I was not a fan of algebra and that did take a lot of tutoring. Statistics was also a bit of a struggle, but I mastered it by the end of the semester. I eventually finished all my prerequisites and applied to the nursing program. When the letter arrived saying that I had been accepted, I cried! They recommend that you do not work while going through the program, but I had to work. I had to figure out a way to balance college, work, and home life.

I continued working full-time while going to college, but I had the support of my husband and family, which made it more doable. I would work all day, take classes at night, and do 12-hour clinicals on the weekends. I would study every chance I got and had very little sleep! I met several great people and formed very deep bonds with my classmates. We had study groups, carpools to clinicals, and were there for each other as much as we could be. You needed a 78% to stay in the program. We lost a few classmates along the way who were unable to keep up with the coursework. I watched them struggle and it terrified me that I would fail, so I pushed even harder. Nursing classes are not easy, and I had to really put in extra time, especially since I had been out of school for so long. I truly did struggle at times, but I was not willing to give up!

I managed to survive and graduated amidst a pandemic. We were denied the opportunity to walk at graduation and did not get a pinning ceremony due to COVID-19, which was devastating for me and my classmates.

I immediately went into bedside nursing during the pandemic; it was brutal. We had so many patients and so little staff. I was exhausted, but knew that this was what I wanted to do. I would not recommend graduating and starting a career during a pandemic, but I have to say it worked out for me. I learned so many things during that time. I had many heartbreaks and triumphs. I feel that it made me a stronger nurse.

I have been in bedside nursing since I graduated, and would not change a thing! I won a Daisy Award for nursing which was an honor, because it is an award to recognize a nurse for going above and beyond. To be such a new nurse and to receive an award like the Daisy Award made all of my late nights, tears, and struggles worth every bit of it.

The only advice that I can give is to never give up! You are not too old to pursue your dream. The more you believe in yourself and push yourself the more you will succeed. I was not the oldest in my class, and yes, it was hard, but I finished, I graduated! I am now out there hopefully making a big difference in people's lives, which is what I have always dreamed of doing. NEVER GIVE UP ON YOUR DREAM!

Karmi Jones

Heart & Harmony Wellness LLC
Life Coach

https://www.facebook.com/profile.php?id=100068881255625

Welcome! The purpose here is to help remind you that YOU matter!
Focusing on you is NOT selfish!

EVERYONE HAS A STORY TO TELL. THIS IS MINE

By Karmi Jones

I grew up with parents who didn't get divorced. Sure, they must have had their fair share of problems, and sometimes I overheard conversations about them, but it wasn't anything extreme. I grew up thinking and knowing that that was what I wanted for myself and my family one day. Now, let it be known that while they were together before, they weren't married until I was eight years old. If my dad hadn't passed away this past spring, they would have celebrated their 30th wedding anniversary.

Abuse and trauma were something I never thought I'd endure. They were words that never entered my head except for on those after-school specials or TV shows where someone suffered physical abuse and it was figured out and "made better" by the next episode, or shortly thereafter. Mental and emotional abuse certainly weren't things that were talked about, or even known about, for that matter. So, far be it for me to think that years later, I'd be the one to experience this firsthand, and from multiple men. But yet it happened. It happened fast and it happened quickly. It happened before I even realized it!

When you get married—sorry, when you start to think about marriage during the height of purity culture, while going to a catholic school and learning about all of that—it honestly doesn't help! I married my third-ever boyfriend and had saved myself for marriage, like a "good girl." While I don't regret anything, as I wouldn't have the life and people I have now, things might have been a little different.

So, I started a family when I was barely 21, and was divorced before I turned 30—with a whole lot of trauma and abuse sprinkled in. This also meant that my knowledge of relationships was limited. Not knowing much about mental and emotional abuse, I had no idea that the friendship (or friend with benefits) that I had after my divorce was going to be FULL of it!

Full of things like being told who to see and who to hang out with, what I was allowed to wear and what I wasn't. If I upset him or did something I "shouldn't" have, I was given the silent treatment and had to "earn back" the "right" to speak to him. After over 10 years of being free from him and over eight years of therapy, the silent treatment STILL triggers me (and "triggers" is not a word I use lightly). I basically had to cut off everyone but him, a couple of other VERY select people (most of whom he didn't even know about), and my son. You also come to realize who your true friends are when you tell them what happened and they either believe you or leave you high and dry and cut you out of their lives completely, no matter how long you've been friends.

After that, I was in a couple of relationships where, for lack of a better term, I was the secret. Not in the sense that no one knew about me, but in the sense that I was dating men who had children and I wasn't allowed or able to meet them (for the record, my "rule" was: If I am going to meet the kids and spend time with them, I want to meet their mom so they knew who I am and feel comfortable with their children being with another female—and I NEVER tried to replace them). As you can imagine, those relationships came with their own sets of issues and trauma, including, but not limited to, feeling like I wasn't ever good enough or the right person for them, being kept a secret, and being walked out on because of a guilt trip put on by another woman.

Then we have the drug-addicted ex-felon, who was NEVER in recovery despite years of saying he was going to meetings and getting treatment for his addiction. With this one, things started going missing, and he blamed it on other people coming into the house. Turns out, he was pawning it all for drug money. Three years later, the final straw was when he stole and totaled my car while driving without a license and then refused to sign the papers to get it out of the impound lot for six weeks. He pawned things like priceless family jewelry, my son's gaming consoles and video games, DVDs, and computers. Little tip for you— if you're dating someone and they say their ex is crazy, but you've met the ex and can't figure it out, DON'T believe them! Chances are very good that the ex is actually the more sane of the two! Turned out that his "crazy ex-wife who is just out for what she can get" is actually one of the sweetest women ever, and I actually became friends with her and stayed a part of the kids' lives! One of the very few good things to come out of this was my decision to become a life coach. I decided to dedicate my life to helping women become phoenixes and rise from the ashes of their previous lives to become new, more confident, improved versions of who they were before!

So here I am, tattered and bruised and worn out and ready to give up, when someone unique and special comes along. When you least expect it, and sometimes, when you're in the thick of it, you find someone who helps you heal. Who sees your faults and scars and turns them into tiger stripes and lessons learned. You find someone who is willing to accept you and your baggage and all they ask in return is for you to accept them and theirs (which may even be less damaging than yours).

More than eight years of therapy and counseling later, I still am not healed. But I will tell you some things I have learned that maybe can help you. Wounds heal, inside and out—the inside ones just take more work, and that's ok! It's ok to set boundaries and prioritize your mental health, as long as you are doing it in a way that's helpful for YOU. Being hurt and wounded isn't a good enough reason to shut the world out, despite what you may think at the time. Life is worth it; there is always someone who will be your grounding point and the person to keep you on this Earth until you feel strong enough to keep yourself here. Therapy isn't something to be ashamed of, we ALL need someone to talk to, no matter the situation or person!

Kathryn Whittington

Ashtabula County Commissioner
Elected Official

https://www.linkedin.com/in/kathryn-whittington-21804a42/
https://www.facebook.com/kathryn.whittington.75?mibextid=LQQJ4d
https://www.instagram.com/vote_kathryn_whittington/

Kathryn Whittington was elected to serve on the Ashtabula County Board of Commissioners on January 3, 2017, for a four year term of office. Commissioner Whittington was re-elected to serve an additional four year term of office to begin on January 3, 2021.

Kathryn has been working diligently since elected on the drug epidemic locally, statewide, and nationally. She has created an initiative, Rural America, and spoken across the country on the prevention efforts and successes of Ashtabula County. Kathryn supports law enforcement and was instrumental in the creation of the new Crime Enforcement Agency of Ashtabula County (CEAAC), a drug task force that serves Ashtabula County.

Kathryn was previously employed with Ashtabula County Children Services, serving the children and families of Ashtabula County for 15 years, and has over 25 years of experience working with families and communities. She was formerly the Community Service Coordinator for Ashtabula County Children Services Board and served as the Interim Chair of the One Ohio Foundation Board.

Kathryn currently serves as the Chair for the Health & Human Services Committee through the County Commissioners Association of Ohio; as the Sub-Committee Vice-Chair for the Human Services and Education Steering Committee through the National Associations of Counties; and as Chair of the One Ohio Foundation Board.

Kathryn is a West Geauga High School graduate and has an Associate's Degree in Business Administration Management and a Bachelor's Degree in General Business Administration.

VICTIM TO VICTORY

By Kathryn Whittington

I never aspired to be a writer. My lifelong dream was to serve others. I write this to truly inspire and support others in the knowledge that they are not alone, they can achieve their lifelong dreams, and they can make a difference. I have faith in humankind and I believe in my community.

My life story is full of adventure. I am a Christian, wife, mom, nana, public servant, speaker, presenter, victim of crime, and an advocate for children and families.

I was raised in the Methodist faith. My faith is my rock when the world is uncertain. I share my faith with my readers and want to show you how big of a role it has played in my life and my successes.

Being a mom and step-mom to five children has been a blessing, but as we all know, we can't always protect them from danger.

October 9, 2013, would turn out to be the most impactful but traumatizing day for me. It was a beautiful morning. The sun was out and the day was going to be one of the last warm days before northeast Ohio would start getting cold weather. I struggled that morning with whether to take the day off or to go in for the lunchtime meeting I had. I made the decision that it would be easier to go in for the meeting than it would be to reschedule.

I left later than usual that morning. Halfway down the road, I realized I had left my iPad behind. I hesitated for a moment but decided I wouldn't need it and continued on to work. During the meeting, my daughter called. I sent it to voicemail. She left me a message that said, "I tried calling the house and now your cell. I am headed to Grandma's." Later this would prove to be an important piece. It is speculated that it was her leaving a message on the house phone saying, "Mom are you home yet?" that rushed the burglars out, thinking I was on my way home.

It was around 3 p.m. when my youngest son called in complete hysteria, yelling that the house had been broken into. I kept him on the phone, called the Sheriff's Department, and let my supervisor know I was leaving and that the house was broken into. I called my husband so that he could leave work and meet me at the house.

It was on this day that I realized the magnitude of the issues caused by the drug epidemic within my community—the impact on law enforcement, the county budget, and the county jail.

The deputy showed up to start the investigation just as I was pulling into my driveway. I was just shocked that everything was gone. Personal items went through. And they broke things. Why break items? If you weren't stealing them, no need to break them so I couldn't use them again. Each room in the house had been gone through. Guns, jewelry, kitchen items, clothing, money, gift cards, electronics, game systems, televisions, and so much more. They even went through my washer and dryer, pulling out all the clean clothes. I'm not sure what other people use their washer and dryer for, but mine is used for the sole purpose of washing and drying clothes. Not hiding my belongings when I leave the house.

See, we had just finished building the house and I had only been in the home for four months. Boxes unpacked made the burglary easy. I had labeled all the boxes. The deputy took the report. Several hours later my iPad was showing at a location about 45 minutes from our house; still in the county. I was certain we would get all of our belongings back. In reality, it had been approximately eight hours since they had been in the house. Our personal belongings were long gone by then. I was angry! I wanted to know WHERE MY STUFF was.

Unfortunately, nothing was recovered that night. That's right, NOTHING recovered, including the iPad. How is that possible? Well, it is.

Feeling victimized, I searched for suspects, my belongings, and answers. Every waking moment was consumed by this crime. I wanted justice and I wanted my stuff back. I started working the case. Apparently, I felt I had watched enough crime television to know how to be a detective. That was the farthest thing from the truth. Though I was not a detective, I still continued to try to connect the dots. Who did this and why? Eventually the who came out. The why I will never know. I will never know if it was targeted or random. Do I need to know? Will it make a difference? The unknown is the part of this equation that keeps me wondering.

A few items would eventually be recovered. The items were found during the investigations of other crimes in the county. To this day, I hold hope that more items will be returned, but I know deep down that that isn't going to happen.

Eventually, we would know who was involved, but only a few would be charged with receiving stolen property and none would be charged with the burglary. I would learn that many would never be charged so that they could be convicted for more serious crimes they had committed. I absolutely couldn't comprehend why they would never be charged. Accepting this was difficult. I am still a little angry about this but I have learned to accept it. It was hard to accept because I do not believe I have received justice for being a victim of a burglary.

As days turned into weeks, I decided it was time to reach out to my county commissioner. The commissioner was aware of the burglary and told me to reach out if there was something I needed. It wasn't my need that drove me to contact the commissioner—it was the issues my community had with a drug epidemic.

My community had a drug problem and a jail issue. The commissioner spent five minutes with me before telling me that my remarks and concerns were not accurate. I left the office and thought to myself, wow, this is not how government should address the genuine concern of a constituent. However, that was the way they handled it, and that needed to change.

The burglary was a turning point in my life, or as some say, the day I was changed forever. I see now why people think that. Everything I do is driven by that one day in October. I say that is the day God put my faith to the test and took me down the path to being a voice that makes a difference. What I wasn't prepared for was what came next.

In August of 2015, I made the decision to run for County Commissioner. I knew that I needed to, instead of being on the sidelines and complaining about what was happening to our community.

In October 2015, I found out that I would have to quit my job of 13 years as a public servant. I was a classified government employee and was not allowed to run for political office as long as I was employed. Without missing a beat, I turned in my resignation the same day—a decision I never regretted.

Having no political experience was not only a bad thing—the bad part was I had to figure out how to run a campaign with zero experience—but a good thing, too. The good was that I would eventually have a handful of experienced people reaching out to help and guide me through the campaign process.

My journey as a candidate was ready to start. Petitions pulled, signatures obtained and turned in to the Board of Elections. Let the campaign begin. Oh my, what was I thinking! I did not realize how difficult it was going to be to put together a campaign committee. This isn't really something that people want to spend endless hours of volunteerism on just so the candidate can hopefully win. A few close friends who believed that I would be a good commissioner and what this county needed ultimately became Team Whittington! I would be A FRESH voice for Ashtabula County.

Since my family has been directly affected by addiction, I have a personal interest in supporting and helping others who suffer from this disease. So, I have taken my journey on the road as a speaker and presenter at drug epidemic forums across the country.

As I sit here today with a child who fights addiction and raising grandchildren, I know that I made the right decision to run for office and help fight the drug epidemic.

There is always hope and you are never alone!

Kerry Gudim

Blessed at One Stop Shop
Online Business Owner / Services Broker

https://www.linkedin.com/in/kerry-gudim-6a25b5205/
https://www.facebook.com/kerry.lynn.5602728
https://www.instagram.com/kerrygudim
https://www.blessedatonestopshop.acnibo.com

Kerry Gudim is a single Mom of three amazing, caring, strong, resilient young men. Grandma to one grandson. She is an online business owner and entrepreneur with a long background in Early Childhood Education, working on the ground level with children and their families. For several years she was the director of a nonprofit daycare centre. She loves to care for children and serve their families. Over the years Kerry has loved to serve others through her church and community by playing musical instruments and singing with praise teams, working with youth, cleaning, running a food bank, sewing quilts for charity, cooking, leading Bible studies, teaching Sunday school and children's church, serving in womens ministries, serving a term on church board, acting in dramas and musicals, choir. Playing music at nursing homes to bring comfort and entertainment to seniors. Acknowledging all gratitude joyful success to her saviour Jesus and support of her family.

PEACE, LOVE, GRACE

By Kerry Gudim

I came to on the floor of our school's library. My head was shooting sharp pains. How did I get here? I felt like a truck had run over me! Carefully pulling myself into a standing position, I checked myself over. No rips in my pants. No carpet burns on my hands and knees. Throbbing head. Woozy stomach. Locking up the library, I headed down the hall to the computer lab to let my two youngest sons know I was ready to take them skating.

While the boys skated, I took stock of how my body was feeling. Not so great. As time passed, I felt more ill and pained. Picking up my cell phone, I called my principal to let her know what had happened and that I was going to head to the hospital. A slow stopping and starting drive home on a cold dark winter's night. A few phone calls after arriving home and a family friend took the three of us to the hospital. Graciously waiting with my boys. My gratitude for this family and the help, care, and prayers they lovingly extended.

Hours later, with a diagnosis of concussion and a recommendation for lots of sleep and to go to a physiotherapist the next day, we headed for home. The journey to healing began.

Hello, my name is Kerry Gudim. My story begins in my 49th year. I am a mom to three amazing sons! Blessed and thankful that God gave me children to parent. I am an Early Childhood Educator and an Educational Assistant. I have had a lifelong career of caring for children and their families, a career I have loved being a part of—getting to observe and listen to the needs of others while coming up with creative solutions to help them have more opportunities to grow and enjoy that time.

Waking up the day after, life felt different. My body and head hurt terribly. I could not see straight or walk straight. I was nauseous. Light was too bright. I was weak and shaky. Sound. Oh my, sound was everywhere, and it just couldn't seem to get quiet enough! Tasks and movements that used to be second nature were like I had never known how to do them, and I was relearning them! Getting ready to go to the physiotherapist later that week was a comedy of catastrophe! Could I bend to put on socks without falling over? Could I reach up to brush my hair? The car ride there was even crazier! I couldn't decide what to hold! My head? My stomach? The door? Closing my eyes! Traffic and the world moved way too fast. The diagnosis after the tests from the first appointment led me to understand that there were many appointments to be had ahead, and that there was help available.

Two weeks later COVID hit our communities, and the schools and businesses began their waves of rules and closures. Homeschooling for my teens and the school I worked at began. Two teens living at home. I wondered and prayed that my adult son and his family would weather it all well.

Blessings rained down abundantly! My parents and friends went out of their way to take me to appointments; driving was off the "can do" list for the time being. Meals arrived on the doorstep, no small feat as our church members and friends created meals that we could eat without having allergic reactions…of which there was a long list to avoid. So very grateful for these special family members and friends! The love and care given to myself and to our family!

Six weeks later. Pitch black in the living room; it's probably after midnight. Trying to find my way across the room and bumping into things, I reach to turn on the cast iron floor lamp. I fell to the floor in a pain-riddled tearful lump! My youngest flew out of his room, turning on the lights. Seeing me, he took off running to sit devastated on the back porch. Devastated that he had accidentally been the cause of the lamp falling to pieces on my head. You see, he had thought out the most AMAZING practical joke ever! He had unscrewed the lampstand pieces and carefully balanced them all atop each other waiting for his brother to receive the joke. I absolutely love a good practical joke—this time the joke was on me! And a second concussion to the opposite side of my head. I have repeatedly tried to convince my son that it was the best joke I have yet to see! If we had it on film, I am certain that it would have won Funniest Home Videos!

As weeks of closures went by and I continued doing my best to heal, life was challenging for our whole family. I was doing my best to meet financial responsibilities as a single separated mom. Learning how to cut with scissors again and to write, to talk without slurring or mixing up my words and numbers, to read and do the math of finances. I was relearning how to walk up and down stairs, go for walks, and other forms of large and small motor movements. By the late spring, I was driving short distances again! I returned to work part-time in the classroom for a month, classes were in session again and I had healed so much! I was so excited to be able to work again.

My first day back was a professional development day—perfect for getting a slow start back in. I was sorting through books to shelve in the library and through puzzles to keep. I found that I was frustrated and disappointed with my body. Things I used to do easily were difficult. I was dizzy, nauseous, and in pain from these simple activities. What used to take me a minute or two was taking me 30 minutes or longer to complete, and with great effort. Throughout my healing process, I thought often of different children I had worked with over the years to help learn the skills I was now relearning. A deepened admiration for what each child had accomplished boomed within me; especially after working in the classroom daily with the children. At the end of that month I was unable to continue. I was having pain that repeatedly sent me to the hospital and I was missing time.

As we neared the end of the school year, the schools were once again closed and we were homeschooling again. One of my sons was taking a construction class; hammering and saws don't mix well with a concussion, so his grandparents offered to help that month. After he completed his courses, we were looking forward to him coming home that next day.

My phone rang and I was expectantly excited for news that family was on the way home. To my horror it was my mother talking shakily from a police station informing me my son was missing. The scariest time imaginable. My son gone. During COVID lockdown in a major city. 12 days of the most helpless feeling. So many people I am grateful for who helped to search for and lead us to our son. The many lockdowns had caused my son's mental health to deteriorate, which I was unable to see the enormity of due to my own healing. 13 days later, when my parents and son walked through the door of my home, a million questions and concerns ran through my mind. I opened my arms wide and hoarsely whispered, "I love you." My son melted in deep sobs in my arms, my own tears flowing freely with his.

After a summer of individual and family counseling, testing for learning needs, several diagnoses made, and more concussion physiotherapy appointments, it was coming time to register the boys for the fall session of school and for me to return to work. My son shared that he wasn't going to return to school; that school was too hard. I sent up a quick prayer and asked him if he would consider staying in school for the next couple of years until he could graduate if I could find a way to stay home and homeschool him myself. He said, "Only if we can do it in one year." I began to search for ways to make this happen. In the meantime, we packed our car to head down to camp at my parents for the weekend for the last campout of the season.

Everyone in the car and off we went! Driving down the highway! A Beautiful field of sunflowers! Flash of blinding light!

My internal dialogue…"Where am I? Whose car is this? Who are these young men in the car? Who am I? I must know how to drive; I'm driving. Where am I going? Ok God, I don't know who I am or anything right now. I'm scared and trusting you to help me." A feeling of peace entered me and I drove a straight path recognizing nothing, blindly trusting God. An hour later the young man in the front seat looked up from reading a book, saying, "Mom! You just drove past our turn!"(Ok! Thank you, Lord! I'm a Mom! These are my kids!) Turning around and following my sons.

"Hey! Moooom! Turn here," until we arrived at his grandparents. I pretended to know my family and did my best to cope with being blank. The next morning, finding a doctor's phone number in my phone, I called my doctor and, with his order to tell the family and get to Emergency, we were on the road with Grandma driving. A long day. A diagnosis of concussion and GTA. I insisted on a referral to a neurologist. Five months later, after endless tests, the neurologist and I met up for the diagnosis in his office.

Sitting across from the neurologist, he shared his diagnosis and thoughts. "Stoic epilepsy. Concussion syndrome. Migraine Syndrome. No further healing." His fingers tented together. He quietly and deeply studied me. "How are you here in front of me? Everything in your test results show you should not be alive. Many times over."

I responded, meeting his gaze unwaveringly. "God has a far greater purpose for my life that I have yet to complete. He is not done with me."

The doctor said, "I don't believe in God."

Continuing to look the doctor in the eyes, I responded with, "But I'm sitting here in front of you." To which the doctor conceded that what I had lived through and my presence in front of him was akin to what even he had no other words for than "It is a miracle." The healing journey and living with the diagnosis has been one of up and down days. Yet mentally and emotionally God has strengthened me and brought our family closer.

Two days before school started for my youngest, God gave me an amazing opportunity with an online Christian homeschool program where they agreed to take it one day at a time with my middle son and me so that he could work toward graduation. Both my youngest and middle son struggled during those months. We spent time in counseling and with him on a suicide watch, caring and praying and teaching. At the end of that school year, my middle son proudly graduated from high school with a grade point average 60% higher than he had had before. He worked so hard! I am so proud of the inner and outer work he has done. He is now an adult out on his own, happily working a career in a field he is excited to work in!

The same two days before school started that fall, I received a phone call from a friend asking me if I could use some help paying my bills…she told me she had a neighbor who might have a solution for me. I agreed to talk with my friend's neighbor. After a presentation and a solid "NO thank you" from me to the solution that I thought would be impossible given all the challenges on our plate, the neighbor left for home. That night, God and I had a Jacob's ladder wrestle. Upon waking the next morning, God asked me, "Why can't you do this? You say you have to keep learning how to do things like cutting with scissors. Why not learn this too?" I could not argue with that! I called my friend's neighbor and asked, "How do I get into this? How do I do this?"

I have now been learning to be a businesswoman. I am doing something I never thought I would do, or for that matter, would be capable of doing. God gave me and my family this gift. It has provided for and given me time to homeschool and be here for my teens. To see them through high school. It had me here when I was most needed. As a single mom, it gave me something I wouldn't have had: time. Time I can never get back. My youngest is in his last few months of high school now and preparing for graduation. My boys are growing into caring, capable young men.

One of my sons recently said to me, "Mom I'm so proud of you! You are like Job. You never say anything against God. You only praise Him and pray to Him. You just keep on going no matter what comes your way! You show me every day that I can do hard things just by watching you!" Tears filled my eyes. Our children are watching, even if we're just doing what we need to to help everyone get through the tough times while showing them love. I am sharing these trials not to glorify them, but to glorify God. God has covered me in blessings of peace, love, and grace during times of unknown journey ahead. He has brought me and my family through difficult times. We have grown stronger. I have healed beyond the capabilities the doctors said were possible. He has given me a new lease on life with a healthier and happier family and self. He has given me a new direction and a way to joyfully serve families with value. Peace. Love. Grace. Gratitude. I am blessed.

Kimberley Collise

Insight Consulting
RN, CLNC, SCRN

https://www.insightconsultingrn.com/

Kim Collise is a Registered Nurse with over 27 years of diverse healthcare experience. With attention to detail, strong communication, and organizational skills, she started her own consulting business in 2007. Kim has always been a strong patient advocate, both at the bedside and beyond the traditional four walls of healthcare. She earned the nicknames "Nancy Drew" and "eagle eyes" due to her refined attention to detail. That genuine passion spills over to nature with any creature that shows up at her doorstep. Yes, they all are fed. Kim has also served Lake County, Ohio on several Boards. When not working hard, Kim can be found visiting her mom, Nancy, reading, traveling, watching mystery shows, or enjoying a white or red at one of the local wineries. Kim currently resides in Perry, Ohio with her fiancée Jason, and furry kids Omar, George, Mr. Greybourne, Andi, Randolph, and Marie.

A PRESCRIPTION FOR SUCCESS

By Kimberley Collise

I dedicate this to my father and mother, Vince and Nancy, who truly are the embodiment of never giving up and of what love really means.

I swear I could see the cavities of my neighbors as a child due to the proximity of the homes. Growing up in Ashtabula, Ohio, I was raised under very different circumstances than most of my friends. I lived in a mobile home, my father worked two jobs, and my mom was totally blind—the trifecta for truly not blending in most of the time. Did I mention that I was all but 5'10" in 6th grade? The annual school photo day was always a trip. I towered over everyone, including the teachers some years. This was by far not your typical childhood. I grew up being the eyes for my mom as she navigated the world newly blind not long after I was born. And another sidebar—I was an only child. To some extent, you could say I was already becoming a caregiver as a child, which would prove to be true as time went by. I knew I had to help others, and I knew I needed more space.

When career day rolled around in junior high, I proudly wore what I called my nurse costume, next to my friends the policeman and accountant. Yes, I still have that photo in my scrapbook. It seemed even then, I knew I was destined for a life of caring for others. Yet I wondered, how in the world would I be able to do this? My parents were by no means rolling in the dough, so I guess my brain was going to have to compensate for that. God help me.

I worked very hard all through my junior high and high school years. To make some cash at age 13, I started to work at our parish on weekends, cleaning, answering the phone, and doing whatever other tasks the priests had lined up for me. This was a great way to learn time and money management.

By my junior year of high school, my parents decided I needed to switch schools. I still have nightmares about the initial transition. Aimlessly walking the halls looking for classes and people, yet going nowhere. I went from a group I had known since kindergarten to knowing only a handful of other students. It was truly harrowing. By today's definition, it would have been a Pepcid/Xanax moment. I thought, "Have I not had enough adversity already? Why is all this happening?"

I continued to work hard in school during the day and in retail in the evenings and on weekends. I graduated 13/167 in my class. Not too shabby, all things considered.

I had been applying to various colleges and was accepted at several. Ultimately, I chose to stay at Kent in Ashtabula and entered the nursing program. No easy feat, as they only took 80 students and I was only 18 with zero nursing experience. Why go to a school that will put me in tens of thousands of dollars of debt when I can get just as great of an education at home?

That summer before I started, I applied for every scholarship known to man. By the end of my degree, I only had to pay for one semester of books. This girl made it out of college with her nursing degree debt-free. It was a gift from God and my parents were so proud. I could not believe it had really happened. All the hard work and dedication paid off. In true Kim fashion, as nothing ever really went off without a hitch, at graduation time, I had an allergy issue. There I was, covered in hives and hopped up on Benadryl. Honestly, can anything be smooth for this chick? Little did I know, all of these challenges and hurdles were building an inordinate amount of resilience that I draw upon to this day.

Now the real fun begins. Who wants to hire a newbie nurse with zero healthcare experience? In 1996, you could not walk into any nursing job. You needed several years' experience either in a nursing home or on a medical/surgical floor in a hospital. I continued working at Wal-Mart (I can pierce ears as a side hustle if need be) while applying for jobs and eventually landed my first one at a nursing home in Portage County.

It was very challenging, to put it mildly. 50 patients and I was the only nurse. In those 12 hours, I felt like a human PEZ dispenser of meds. I didn't eat much and may have only gone to the bathroom twice in those 12 hours. Crying nightly became my new pastime. Can I do this? Will it get easier? I continued working, and had amazing mentors. They encouraged me and gave me many tips and tricks they had learned through the years. After one year, I was promoted to Unit Manager. The Director of Nursing noted my dedication, organization, and desire to make things better. It was an amazing year and they wanted me to stay and take the lessons learned to other units. I stayed for another year until I moved back to Lake County, to be closer to my parents in Ashtabula. Lord knows they were the only reason I did not relocate to a warmer place. I swear I was a Southern girl in a past life.

Over the next many years, I worked in different hospitals and nursing homes. Eventually, I graduated to another day shift position where I remained for several years. As I went through shift after shift, I started to remember how much I loved to read and do research. These hobbies went by the wayside after college as I did not want to read anything after all my nursing classes. Just thinking about reading was off the table. My brain was simmering. How do I combine my experience with these other components of my brain? I was just not feeling completely fulfilled even though I loved what I did.

One day I received an unexpected letter. It was my dad's aunt; she had passed away, leaving in her will a small amount of money for us. I was dumbfounded. We were the only family that ever visited her, and even then, it was not that frequent. I was touched beyond words.

That small gift from the heavens was what I used to embark on my first nursing certification. There would have been no other way to achieve that milestone were it not for that gift.

The rest is pretty much history, continuing to work as a registered nurse in various parts of Ohio and in several contract roles. Even though I was not always patient-facing, I was an advocate for those who needed one. I went on to obtain my second certification, being one of the first several in Ohio, and in the United States as well. I also finally upgraded to a two-acre parcel of land where I can decompress and enjoy nature.

There are still moments when I just pause and think, "How did I get here?" It was by no means on my own. I had great parents to support and encourage me, wonderful mentors in healthcare, and the best friends a girl could ask for. There was never a moment when I felt comfortable with the status quo, or with someone telling me this was as good as it gets. I had a vision and I knew what I wanted. I did not want the struggles that I watched my parents endure. They did not want that for me either.

At every step, I thought things over, researched, and evaluated how a decision could impact me in that moment as well as in the future. I knew that I did not have Mom and Dad Warbucks to bail me out if I failed. If anything, I had to be as responsible as possible to care for them if they needed me. There was no parachute, no bail-out. It was all on me. No pressure. Yeah, right!

In hindsight, there were many pearls of wisdom along the way, but the most important one was that I should believe in myself and that I knew what was best for me. My faith In God also became refined through all these scenarios. Without him, none of this would be possible.

No dream is too great when you believe in yourself. The key is to never give up and when you least expect it, your life will change in amazing ways. You just have to keep an open heart and mind. A good sense of humor helps, too. If you thought my childhood and nursing journey were entertaining, you should inquire about my personal life. Now that is reality show-worthy, or maybe a stand-up comedy skit in Vegas. You would have to be the judge.

Godspeed on your journey to your best self. Today could be the day you have always dreamt about; don't blink, or you could miss it!

Renee Molzon

Founder of Renee R Molzon Counseling LLC

https://www.linkedin.com/in/renee-molzon-lisw-s-3830208
https://www.facebook.com/molzoncounseling
https://www.molzoncounseling.com

Renee is a Licensed Independent Social Worker who has grown in this field for over 25 years. She founded Renee R Molzon Counseling, LLC in 2018 while employed full time as a Behavioral Health Social Worker in a community hospital. She began her practice to assist adults who feel powerless over their circumstances and need some extra support to find their strength.

Renee developed her skills and approach by working in various milieus and with clients of diverse ages and backgrounds who have unique needs. Proving that "we are never too old," she enrolled in graduate school at age 47 to further her career. Recently, her passion for grief and trauma work has become the focus of her practice. Her goal is to help others walk through pain and loss to Find The Best Path to Themselves.

JOURNEY TO YOUR BEST SELF

By Renee Molzon

"Girls get married and have children; they don't go to college." This is what I was told at a very young age. Many of you may have heard the same mantra. I was raised during the height of the Women's Liberation Movement by a woman who was raised during the Great Depression and World War II. The generation gap between us was more of a chasm. My mom was a wonderful mother in many ways, don't get me wrong. We were loved and spoiled (as best as they could spoil us because we were also poor) and allowed to be children while we were children. My brother was encouraged to play sports, prepare for college, hang out with his friends—"boys will be boys"—and work jobs; I was encouraged to embroider, learn to clean the baseboards, wash dishes, and wear makeup "just so," with no thought of the future.

In my heart, I did not want to be a wife or a mother. At 12 years old I wanted to become a child psychologist. I pictured myself in a penthouse with a grand car and a stunning wardrobe, helping children be their best selves. At home, I was told to wait on my brother, get him something to drink, see if he wanted seconds of dinner just as my mom did for my dad. Mom was a wonderful wife and mother, and I loved her, but I was being denied the option to be my Best Self at the time by not knowing that I had a choice of what to do. I did not plan for the future as my friends did because "girls don't go to college." I was not taught to budget money—my husband would do that, I was told. The sad part is my mother hated being a housewife. She hated to cook, bake, and take care of the house. She had done that as a child and was over it. Mom had been a draftsperson in the 50s and 60s. She shared many stories of her pride in being one of the few females in the field. She became bitter disclosing that she had to quit when she got pregnant. She stated that she wanted children, but she enjoyed working. Mom was unfulfilled in her life. "This is a woman's lot in life. We let men do what they want, and we don't complain," she would lecture. She meant this in all the ways that you are thinking. Her way of protecting me from the pain of having to quit a job I would love was to teach me to have no expectations about life.

I complained. I complained loudly and often. Oh, I would not want to have lived with me during those years. I wanted more! I had a drive to be more and do more. I had a desire that was in complete opposition to the way I was raised. I wanted to be my Best Self without understanding why, how, or that it was even possible. But what is our Best Self, and how do we become that? Is the concept of Best Self to be in one or multiple areas of our lives? Do we view it spiritually, philosophically, or by tangible accomplishments? There are many definitions of Best Self: the ability to work toward your goals; living authentically; being capable; making sure you're doing what brings you a sense of happiness, purpose, and meaning; understanding and unlocking your potential. This sounds like a tall order. Writing this, I am struck with Imposter Syndrome. What have I done to qualify me to speak on this subject? Am I even *my* Best Self? How will I know?

There is an archetype that divides a woman's life into three stages: The Maiden, The Mother, and The Crone. I feel that in each stage we use the experiences (feelings) we have and the knowledge that we have learned to be our Best Self. Our idea of Best Self can, and should, change as we grow and evolve. How did I become my Best Self throughout those different stages? There were times when my Best wasn't so good. Middle school and teenage years are examples of "not so good." How many of us were bullied in middle school? I wore glasses, hand-me-downs, and thrift store clothing. I had to wear special (read "hideous") shoes due to medical issues. My hair was not "styled," it was long and stringy. I had the trifecta of a bully's targets. Oh, and I was "one of the smart kids." I hated middle school. High school wasn't much better for me; I'll spare you the details.

I did get to go to college—community college—and then, because I did well and received my Associate of Arts degree, I was able to take out loans and attend state school to get my Bachelor of Arts in Psychology. But I stopped there, as I was still waiting for my prince to ride up and drag me by my hair to toil in his home forever (I mean "marry me and make me happy"). Looking back, I see my Best Self at the time as a hardworking young adult. I had many jobs during school: fast food, retail, waitressing, dispatching, all jobs that brought out my personality and my confidence. This solidified in me that there was something more for me out there. I enjoyed people and I was good at engaging them. But the old tapes kept playing…"You should be married, you are not good enough to work, you are not cut out for anything big, stay under the radar."

My first experience seeing a therapist was at about 26 years old. We delved into the idea that I might be "good." It may be okay to find my own idea of Best Self and not follow what my family thinks it should be. We worked on my self-confidence, discussed limiting beliefs, and reframed my automatic negative thoughts. I was working at a job I loved, I had friends, and I had my own home. At that stage of life, I was my Best Self. Time passed, as it does, and life happened. I was interviewing for my dream job in Texas and my father became ill. I stayed put and took a job out of my field to be my Best Self as a daughter.

Eventually I got married and helped raise two stepchildren. That was a difficult transition for me, from single 34-year-old to instant family. Not my Best Self for many of those years, let me just say. But we all survived, and hopefully I had some positive impact on the children. I went back for my master's degree. I had many people encouraging and supporting me, especially my husband. I graduated three months before my 50th birthday. While in school we had to move Mom out of her house. My brother and I split time with her. I changed jobs during that time as well. I was so very overwhelmed, but in hindsight, I did the best I could. I also asked for help when I needed it.

In 2018, I had had enough of being treated poorly at my job and decided to start my own business. I had absolutely no idea what I was doing! Luckily, a friend was willing to rent me an office for a reasonable price and was a wonderful cheerleader and mentor. After two years, I was able to quit my other job and solely work at my private practice. Was it easy? Heck no! Did I lose sleep? So much! Was it worth it? Most definitely! I can't imagine anything else. Am I my Best Self? For the moment, yes. I am constantly evolving and learning. I believe that that is part of being your Best Self; to understand that there is always more to learn and a different way to do things.

Here are a few of the things I've learned so far:

1. When God, or the Universe, wants you to change, your life will become so uncomfortable you have no other choice.
2. Ask for and accept help. You do not need to do anything on your own.
3. You do have what it takes to see your dreams come true.
4. We all must start somewhere, and we don't know anything when we start.
5. Change is scary.
6. You will make mistakes because you are human. No one gets it all right the first time.
7. Friends are important.
8. Each failure is a learning opportunity.
9. You are worth it, and you deserve it.
10. It is just as easy to think positively.

And finally,

Living by your values and beliefs will always make you your Best Self. There can be no happiness if we do not follow our truth. Trust yourself, love yourself, and take the risks. You got this!

Suzanne E Minshew

Founder of Zannie Goods

https://www.facebook.com/sminshew/
https://www.instagram.com/zannie_minshew/
https://www.findingyourhealing.com/

Suzanne is a wife, mom of three, and grandma to two, and loves her family and the Lord beyond measure. She has a BA from Hiram College and has had a successful career in management, recruiting, and career coaching as well as healthcare, with smatterings of volunteer work focused primarily on fundraising. Throughout her career she has been afforded the opportunity to do extensive amounts of writing, from standard orders of procedure and company policies to employee hero stories and media releases. A true entrepreneur at heart, she focuses her work time on her online business, writing, and developing multiple streams of income, including a new blog, Finding Your Healing, that focuses on grief and loss. She is a firm believer in being a lifelong learner, so in her leisure time, you can often find her working around her home and property, listening to YouTube videos on her newest endeavor.

LIVING MY BEST LIFE

By Suzanne E Minshew

I could tell you a tale of a perfect youth, amazing success in college, a flawless career, marriage, children, and an ultimately perfect life, but that is not real, accurate, or honest for me, nor for most people. I see living my very best life as celebrating my successes, learning from my failures, and working tirelessly to live a beautiful and fulfilling life. While I was formerly an optimist, I now tend to err on the side of realism, allowing myself to ebb and flow with the tides of life, understanding that if a rip tide hits, I need to resist fighting, relax, and allow the current to release me when it is ready—or face great suffering. This has been a great lesson for me.

As a child, I was powerless over everything, except my mind and bodily functions, so I learned at an early age to succumb to the will of my mother (a closet alcoholic) and the other adults in charge of me. As a teen and young adult, I struggled with depression, inadequacy, and low self-worth. I thrived on stage, which allowed me to be anyone else but the ugly, awkward me, and found my greatest comfort in music and writing. I listened to music that evoked strong emotion, I sang in choir and in theater, and I wrote poetry and articles for the school newspaper and yearbooks. Those were my escapes and I survived.

As a young adult in college, I unknowingly began the desperate search to tend to the trauma and unattended emotions created during my upbringing. I was broken in so many ways, using alcohol, wandering aimlessly. I was unable to have a healthy relationship because, truthfully, I was an immature child with many deficits, and I simply didn't know how. Fast forward to the pinnacle moment that caused me to surrender: I had burned bridges and failed at or simply walked away from just about everything. I turned away from people who wanted to help. I did not feel worthy of love, acceptance, or anything good. I didn't want to live. Enter a guy who said all the right things—I had known him when I was in high school. He cheated on me then, but why did I deserve anything better? After a year of drinking, being abused on many levels, and finally becoming pregnant, I was at my lowest. I did my best to do the right thing by staying with the guy, but came to the realization that I wouldn't survive to raise my child, so I begged my mother to come home. I was broken, and with complete surrender to our heavenly Father, months of intensive therapy, multiple 12-step programs, legal battles, work, and finishing up the college degree that I had abandoned three classes away from graduating, I was the healthiest and happiest I had ever been in my short lifetime.

I tell you this not for pity or shock, but to share with you the story that has led me to the full and vibrant life I get to live today, some 30 years later. My truth is that, were it not for those tumultuous times, realization, surrender, and healing, I would never be where I am today. So for that, I am grateful. God has truly carried me through and healed parts of me that I had no idea needed healing.

Over the years my relationship with depression and low self-esteem has changed. I have become aware that when I have those times of sinking into nothingness or the negative thoughts start creeping in, that is the darkness trying to rob me of the joy, happiness, and contentment that I so richly deserve. This awareness leads to action and because I am a sensitive soul, I tend to be gentle with myself as necessary. When I feel depression creeping in, I listen to uplifting music, usually Christian music because who really has had it worse than Jesus? I take a bath, so good; walk, preferably with a change of scenery from my neighborhood; talk with a friend or my husband; work out, because endorphins; write, which gives me freedom; read my bible, I find so much love in those pages; or do something kind for someone else.

Whatever makes the depression slink away like the coward he is and allows healing to present itself.

When the negative thoughts start to bombard my brain I have to be more aggressive. Thought-stopping is a handy tool I learned from my first therapist. When a negative thought comes in, stop it in its tracks. Visualize a wall, a sinkhole, blowing it up, whatever works for you. Then, although I sometimes forget, I compliment myself on a job well done and replace that negative thought with a positive thought or self-affirmation, because we all deserve to hear the good things about ourselves.

Relationships with others have been a learning opportunity. My first relationship, with my mother, was filled with guilt, shame, and secrets, which set the tone for how I handled all relationships in my life. Being extremely naive, I have difficulty discerning safe from unsafe people, unless it is blatantly clear, so I have had both come and go in my life. I'm always learning, albeit sometimes painful lessons. Healing myself, the relationship with my mother, and working to heal all of my hurts and hang-ups, I ultimately achieved the blessing of being able to forgive her for her part and to forgive myself for all the relationship blunders I created, which was the greatest gift I could have given myself.

I look back and see that the Lord has blessed me with wonderful relationships despite my brokenness: childhood friends who kept me busy; my high school friend group, who saved me from a teen life of drugs, alcohol, and pregnancy; college friends who saved me from myself time and time again; an older brother, who I didn't grow up with after the age of 5, but has provided clarity and insight to fill in many of the gaps and is truly my best friend; my husband (a mental health therapist—God's sense of humor), who has been patient, loving, and encouraging throughout our 27 years together; and the countless friends I have been touched by with listening ears, kind words, sage advice, laughter, and, at times, utter nonsense. All of these folks have helped me to heal and become a better me, a better wife, mom, friend, and grandma.

The freedom of healing, my undying love of the Lord, and the gifts of my people have been the ultimate opportunity to live my best life. Freedom to tap into my old loves, music and writing; finding new loves, such as riding motorcycles, sewing, hiking, gardening, and running an online business. The freedom to surrender myself daily to the Lord because my issues can resurface at any time and if I don't surrender, they will leak out and deny me the gift of living a beautiful and full life. The freedom to actively work on my relationship with my husband because, aside from God, he is my partner and most important relationship. The freedom to love and care for my adult children from a distance, model healthy boundaries, and provide guidance when asked, and the total freedom to love, tickle, and giggle with my two little grandsons. The freedom to be flexible and reinvent my business when I see trends that show a downturn. The freedom to allow a group of Jesus-loving women to take me into their fold, show me the love of Christ each and every day, and encourage and build me up so that I can be used by the Lord as He sees fit.

There is no magic cure for the ugliness of this world, but we can make our corner of the world beautiful and share it with all those we encounter. Live your best life by casting pride aside, tending to your issues, getting help if you need it, and loving yourself enough to trust the Lord to guide you on His path for you. There will be stumbling blocks, trials, and pain, but the freedom and joy that come as a result is magnificent! Wake each morning with the attitude of leaving the troubles of yesterday where they belong—in the past—and embracing the clean slate of the day to paint a beautiful picture to be entered into your book of life. Pick a life verse for yourself and say it to yourself every day. Pick a song or a podcast that is inspirational and motivational to get your day started on the right foot. Find people who will shore you up so that when things get tough, you are strong. Forgive yourself for mistakes along the way. Challenge yourself daily. Applaud your successes. Most importantly, feel the joy, feel the strength pulsating through you, live in expectation of all that is good and right. Feel yourself living your best life!

Tia J Lawrence

Torchlight Youth Mentoring Alliance
Executive Director

https://www.facebook.com/tia.p.lawrence?mibextid=PtKPJ9
https://www.instagram.com/torchlight_yma/
https://www.torchlightyouthmentoring.org/

Tia has worked for Torchlight Youth Mentoring Alliance for 18 years. She started at the agency as a Site-Based Program Manager. In 2015 Tia transitioned to Director of After School Programs for a year before becoming Director of Programs. Tia became Interim Executive Director before officially becoming Executive Director in spring of 2022. Tia received her B.S. degree in sociology from Lake Erie College in 2000. She's a graduate of Leadership Lake County Community Builders Program in 2015 and of the Leadership Lake County Signature Class of 2016. Tia previously sat on the Camp Sue Osborn Board and currently sits on the Lake Geauga Head Start Board and One Step At A Time Lake County Board. She's honored to be leading the Torchlight Team in its mission to foster the development of youth to reach their highest potential as responsible, caring, and adaptable young adults.

TRUST IN YOURSELF AND BE OK WITH NO

By Tia J Lawrence

In 2005 my oldest daughter had just turned one, and I had been a stay-at-home mom with her up to that point. While I loved being home with her, I knew I wanted to return to the workforce, at least part-time. As if God had a plan for me, I happened to be looking at the newspaper (I know I am dating myself, and am old) and saw a job ad for Big Brothers Big Sisters of Northeast Ohio, now Torchlight Youth Mentoring Alliance. I had always wanted to get involved with the agency as I liked their mission and what they did. On a whim, I sent in my resume, and soon received a call to go in for an interview. During the interview I remember feeling like it was going well, and that I had connected with the women who were conducting it. After not hearing from them for a week, I was disappointed and thought I had not gotten the job. My husband urged me to call and inquire, so I did, and the rest is history.

I have been with Torchlight Youth Mentoring Alliance for eighteen years now. I started as a part-time Site Base Program Manager and I loved it! I worked with kids of all ages and held that position until 2015, when I became Director of Site Base Programs. The following year I was offered the position of Program Director, which I accepted. I was still working part-time, but my work schedule increased in hours. I was so grateful to be able to have a flexible schedule. My husband worked third shift and it was hard trying to find a balance between being a mom and working, and not feeling guilty if I wasn't able to do everything. If I had to miss something for work because of something going on with my family, I would second guess whether I made the right decision, and vice versa if it was something for my family instead of something with work. I would feel extremely guilty and beat myself up about it.

At the end of 2021, my boss informed us all that he was stepping down and asked if I would step into his role as interim director. His leaving was a complete surprise and I was not prepared to step into a full-time position. However, I truly love what we do, and I had faith that God led me to this path for a reason. In December of 2021, I stepped in as interim director and went from part-time to full-time. My kids were older and were involved in various extracurricular activities, but having three kids meant there was always something. Our agency serves three counties in Northeast Ohio: Lake, Geauga, and Ashtabula, which means there is always a meeting, fundraiser, or event. The first year I took over and went full-time, I tried to put my all into work events, and at the same time, attempted to still be at all of my children's activities. I also was trying to keep up with basic house cleaning, which for me was a lot, as I tend to be OCD with cleaning. And then making dinner every night during the week. Exhausting, to say the least!

After the first year, I realized that I don't need to be at everything, and I can not do everything! I know that as women, we put so much pressure on ourselves to do it all, and it is just not fair. This past year I have gotten better at accepting that the house doesn't have to be spotless, and it is ok if there are a few things on my kitchen counter (although it still drives me crazy). I have been better about not having as much guilt if I am not able to be at everything for work, or if I miss a game of my child's because of something at work. It isn't always easy, and the guilt is still there, but I am getting better at not letting it eat at me. I think my advice to people would be to trust their gut. If you feel deep down that it is more important to be at your child's game instead of a networking event, go to the game. I have also learned to have faith and surround myself with good people. I am blessed to have wonderful coworkers who step up for, support, and help one another.

Best Version of YOU

DREAM. BELIEVE. ACHIEVE.

Are you looking for a group of like minded, supportive, and strong women? Are you looking for ways to grow and become the best version of you?

1. **Join our Facebook group** for daily support and community! https://www.facebook.com/groups/bestversionyougroup

2. Share your story! Everyone has a story; you have made it this far and you will help someone. Are you ready to help someone? **Sign up to become a best selling author**!

3. Looking to finally take that step toward being the best version of you and reaching your goals? **Sign up for private coaching**, a plan created to fit your needs and your goals!

4. Ready to make life changes on your own schedule and time? Maybe not want individual coaching but want to start that life-changing process? Announcing the award winning 12- week coaching program! **Sign up for Wavemakers**, using the DBA (Dream, Believe, Achieve) system to start our journey.

So...are you worth it? Don't you deserve to be happy?

There are options to take action. Reach out for a discovery call and let's decide which is the best fit for you.

https://pamkurt.com/
https://bestversionyou.com/
https://www.instagram.com/best_version_you
https://www.facebook.com/bestversionyou/
https://www.linkedin.com/in/pamela-kurt-41a26ba/

Made in the USA
Columbia, SC
27 May 2024

35831321R00054